PRAISE FOR *Aging in High Heels*
THE BOOK AND THE BLOG

A joy, every page... You have so much to share. No one really knows who we are until we put it into words. You are a fabulous writer. You took me right into your heart and soul...your fear and struggles. You will help and inspire so many people. Beautiful!

LINDA EVANS, star of *Dynasty* and author of *Recipe for Life*

Aging in High Heels should be read by women from their twenties and beyond. It's got all the tools that women need to achieve longer, sexier, and more passionate lives!

JUDY FOREMAN, journalist

Beverlye Hyman Fead is an 81-year-old force of nature whose book is brimming with inspiration and good advice on how to face aging well. She has taught scores of individuals to be proactive in their health care, as she herself has been in her own fight against cancer. Her book is a lesson for the ages, for all of us who are fortunate enough to be aging.

SUSAN PESCHIN, President and CEO, Alliance for Aging Research

No matter how old we are, you make it cool to get even older! Your attitude and observations in life, with your particular perspective, are so darned charming! You are one of the special ones who choose to be wide awake... and it's beautiful!

RACHEL MCLISH, former Ms. Olympia
and author of *Flex Appeal* and *Perfect Parts*

Amen to aging with fervor. Here's to all the women of a certain age in the world who aren't famous or even well known who are doing what they have always done, no matter their age. I love how you say, "This is eighty today."

PERIE LONGO
PhD, poet, therapist, and author of *Baggage Claim*

Yours is an amazing story, full of humility and spunk and old Los Angeles history—you bring a forgotten Beverly Hills alive—you bring communities of women into focus—you do so much and you do it with the nuance that makes you the woman everyone wants to know, befriend, marry, be their mother, grandmother, put her art in their rooms.

ALICE RANDALL, songwriter and author of
Soul Food L

Aging in
High Heels

Aging in High Heels

Living a Life with Passion, Hope & Laughter

BY

Beverlye Hyman Fead

Ridgedale Press

2016

ISBN 978-0-692-57458-4

PUBLISHED BY RIDGEDALE PRESS

Santa Barbara, California

Other books by Beverlye Hyman Fead

I Can Do This. Living With Cancer

Nana, What's Cancer?

TYPESET IN MONOTYPE BASKERVILLE

Book & Cover Design by
John Balkwill, Lumino Press

To the members of my family who never had the opportunity to "age in high heels," and to those who are carving new boundaries every day and allowing us to see a glimmer of the future—how to be in charge of our own life as we age.

Contents

Acknowledgments

I'd like to thank the Bronson Foundation for support in making this book a reality.

Thank you to my son, Jim Hyman, his wife, Leslie, and their sons, Alex and Gideon, for always encouraging me and helping to underwrite this book. Thank you to my daughter, Terry Hyman Hamermesh, and her daughter, Tessa, for always cheering me on and helping to launch this book.

Thanks to all my friends, who kept suggesting I turn my blog into a book and spurred me on during the writing of the book. To them I say I so appreciate all your ideas and interest.

I'm grateful to Joan Tapper, my editor, for her interest in my project, her support, and hand-holding throughout the journey. We had many roads to choose, and she helped me choose them. She was good at her craft, egoless, and fun. I thank her from the bottom of my heart.

To John Balkwill, thank you for your beautiful design work and your lovely easy demeanor. You gave the book the panache it needed. It was a pleasure to work with you.

Thank you to my village of doctors who have kept me alive so diligently.

Many thanks to Kim Rojas for her sweet smile, encouragement, and many hours of support while working on this with me. I could not have done this without her.

Thank you to Kim Tom who has worked with me toward this book since the beginning and has always helped me with her interest, her good heart, and her suggestions.

To my grandchildren, thank you for being my constant inspiration in all that I do. I'm so proud of you.

To my husband, who is there for me to read to, to question, to get his guidance and suggestions, and who is constantly telling me I can do this—to him I give my thanks, my love, and my heart.

I also want to acknowledge The Cancer Foundation of Santa Barbara for their financial support and encouragement. I have seen the good works of the Cancer Foundation first hand, and their partnership with the Cancer Center has provided huge benefits to our community.

The mission of the Cancer Foundation of Santa Barbara is to ensure superior cancer care for all citizens of Santa Barbara County regardless of means. To this end, the Cancer Foundation is the leading nonprofit fundraising and grant-making institution dedicated to cancer care in Santa Barbara County and the largest donor to the Cancer Center of Santa Barbara with Sansum Clinic, the leading provider of cancer care on the central coast. Thanks to the extraordinary support of our community and friends, the nonprofit Cancer Foundation and the Cancer Center of Santa Barbara have made a profound impact on those touched by cancer since being founded in 1949.

Introduction

I HAVE BEEN AND CONTINUE to be lucky in my life. I've known the love of a wonderful man and had beautiful children and fabulous grandchildren as well. I have also been involved in and loved art in many different forms—dance, drawing, oil painting, designing ceramics, interior design, photography, and writing. I was given a death sentence (medically) and have lived to laugh it in the face. I was fortunate enough to be in the right place at the right time with the right doctors, just as new treatments were coming into play. With all that luck, however, comes a responsibility: to reach others, give them a hand up, and help them realize what they can do. I am proud to bear that responsibility.

Since I started writing my blog a few years ago, aging seems to have taken on a whole new meaning. At first I thought I would just write about the human side of aging, my personal feelings and experiences. I have lived some eighty years, including more than a dozen with Stage IV cancer, so that gives me some credibility not only as a cancer survivor but also as someone who is aging. I don't consider myself an authority or a writer per se. But I am someone who feels very deeply about things and feels a compulsion to write my thoughts down. If that makes me a writer, then so be it.

I was brought up in California where youth is king. Did I ever think I would be interested in what happens to "older people"? No! I was busy getting tan. But then life happened, and in a blink I became one of those "older people" myself. So not only did I become fascinated by aging, but I also wanted to write about it. The feedback I got for my blog was so gratifying that I wanted to learn and hear more and more. Readers age fifty and up were writing me and saying, "Did you get inside my head? That's just how I'm feeling." I felt a real connection and realized we all needed to know what others thought as they aged. And we needed to think about what was going to change because of our longer lives.

Recently I was invited to speak in Washington at a briefing given by the Alliance for Aging Research (AFAR), the American Association for Cancer Research, and the Personalized Medicine Coalition. Directly after that, I was asked to sit in on a conference on aging, and I came away with some mind-blowing information.

In Washington, the words on everyone's lips were healthspan (rather than just lifespan) and Silver Tsunami—the phrase for the Baby Boomers who will turn eighty in fifteen years. They could wreck the economy if we don't push back age-related diseases—think diabetes, strokes, and heart problems—by eating properly and exercising. The aim for all of us should be to stay healthy all through our life, instead of being sick and fragile the last five or ten years.

My generation is the first of its kind: We are definitely "The New Old."

Well into our eighties we have reinvented ourselves, started businesses, married, and run marathons. We can very well live through our nineties if we are lucky, so we need to make sure these are productive, enjoyable, healthy years.

We can begin by being kind, helping the next person, reading a good book, mentoring a child, starting a new endeavor, or hopping on a plane to a place we've always dreamed of going. Do whatever on this earth interests you.

Aging eventually happens to everyone, so I say let's all "Accept, Adjust and Move On"!

Aging in
High Heels

1
The New Old

To me, wearing high heels is a symbol of not giving in to stereotypes of aging. It's an attitude: "I'm here for a while and don't want to be ignored. I'm still feminine, I'm still relevant, and I'm still vital!"

Things are so different today than they were in your mother's day and definitely very different than they were in my mother's day. We are the "New Old." We're people who keep redefining and reinventing ourselves. We live longer and are in better shape than any generation before us.

Still, aging is complicated, especially when there is a little Stage IV cancer thrown in, as there is in my case. A little case of cancer is like being a little pregnant. But everyone has *something*, don't they? That's what aging is, right?

I have so many feelings about growing older that I want to want to share, such as my insights about living with cancer or any other life-threatening disease. I was told I had two months to live, and here I am years later...feeling great! I have been blessed.

I felt Emile Zola spoke to me when he said, "If you ask me what I came into this world to do, I will tell you; I came to live out loud." So put on your high heels and walk alongside me while we all grow older (not old), wiser, and live out loud together.

Icons

I picked up the Sunday edition of the *Los Angeles Times*, and there it was. The front page of the Image section had a huge photo of...no, not one of the Kardashians but Iris Apfel in all her glory.

Iris is a ninety-three-year-old accessories designer and a true fashion maven who is not only the subject of a coffee table book but also of a new documentary called, appropriately, *Iris*.

What is happening here? Are people beginning to value aging? I think it's that women of a certain age are having their day. Their beauty, their wisdom, their moxie are all ringing out loud and clear! How exciting to be alive and well in such a time!

Ask Ruth Bader Ginsburg, age eighty-two, Associate Justice of the Supreme Court of the United States. Or Carmen Dell'Orefice (known professionally as Carmen), the tall, elegant eighty-three-year-old fashion model. She has more jobs now than she has ever had. Ask Joan Didion, the celebrated eighty-year-old author who happened to be the 2015 face of the French brand Celine, or sixty-nine-year-old actress Helen Mirren, and Twiggy, age sixty-five, who are in ad campaigns for L'Oréal Paris.

In October 2014 *New York* magazine declared, "After 80, some people don't retire. They reign."

How delicious. The magazine cites ninety-two-year-old, ever youthful Betty White and powerful eighty-two-year-old senator Dianne Feinstein. They've still got it! How many more examples do we need?

Aging is simply not what it used to be. If we take good care of ourselves, exercise, eat healthfully—and are lucky—we can go on to live wonderful and productive lives through our nineties. I'm signing up right now!

Eighty isn't the new sixty. This is simply eighty today.

Scaling Down in Style

It was time for my husband, Bob, and me to scale down in our life, but could we actually do it? No more extra closets or extra rooms? Could we give up back-yard parties? Yes, it was time to free ourselves. "Age appropriate," we said to each other. So after twenty-nine years we sold our last house in Montecito and committed to this plan.

We didn't want to leave Montecito, though. We loved it dearly, and it has been an important part of our lives. We still had to be in Los Angeles part-time for Bob's work but no longer wanted or needed a "spread." We looked at everything small: houses, condos…anything we could redo.

We were boarding a plane for a trip to New York when I got a call from my realtor, Rebecca. She was whispering into the phone, "Beverlye, I think I found it for you. I strongly suggest you think about buying this! No redoing, no responsibilities. Sound good?"

Good? Well, actually it's better than that: It's great! We bought a two-bedroom condo in a beach community in Montecito. Set in a glen of trees, it had been gutted and beautifully redone. I love the inside of the condo. But the absolute kicker is that when I walk out my front door I'm roughly a half block from the beach.

Beverlye with her beloved rocks.

When I first saw the place and walked to the ocean, I felt as though I had opened the blinds to the Emerald City of Oz. My new neighbors were going to be birds and dolphins! The green bluffs had trails that bloomed with yellow flowers, and there's sand, rocks, and water—all of my favorites.

I took the yellow brick road down to the beach

where playful dogs were sunning, running, and jumping out of sheer joy at the water's edge, and I felt like doing the same. Anacapa Island sat solidly in the background, while paddle boarders went gliding by, as if in their own silent movie. It was busy and serene at the same time. I could sit on a large rock, and inspiration would just come to me.

Finally, I put on my earplugs and got moving. As Aretha sang "Respect," I walked in time to the music. Every once in a while I spelled it out loud with her— "R.E.S.P.E.C.T., that is what he has for me!!" It was perfect!

The tide was low, and I could walk for hours, past the site of the old Miramar Hotel, past the sweet little beach cottages with their "for rent" and "private beach" signs and their American flags waving proudly. Birds skimmed the water in perfect formation, their whites and grays blending above the blue of the water. The whole scene made my heart happy. This was going to be a great third chapter.

Five Things...

Betty Friedan says, "Aging is not lost youth but a new stage of opportunity and strength." Actually, for me it's five things. Aging is:
1. Inevitable
2. Hard
3. Laughable
4. Melancholy
5. Bittersweet

Here are also five things we do:

1. Go to doctors' appointments. Let's face it, Post Baby Boomer (PBB) social life revolves around doctors' appointments. This is how it works: "Which doctor are you seeing today?" I ask my husband.

"I think it's a stress test," he answers.

"Are you seeing a doctor today?" he asks me.

"Yes, I've got a ENT appointment. Want to have lunch first?"

"Perfect," he says.

Sometimes we fit in breakfast before the appointment or two and sometimes see a movie afterward. That's how it works. Welcome to our PBB world.

2. Eat dinner early! We've all heard the jokes about the "early bird special" and swore it would never be us. But here we are at home, both hungry at 6 p.m. So we eat. What's the big deal? If we go out to dinner with friends, we stretch it to 7:30 p.m. That's a big night. And, yes, we've even occasionally had a late breakfast, no lunch, and a 4:30 EBS dinner... and we loved it!

3. Go to the 4:40 p.m. movie. Self-explanatory and a slam dunk. Movie at 4:40, dinner at 7:00, home and in bed by 8:45. Our favorite night!

4. Be there for each other! There is no competition or judgment. We only want our mates and our friends to be well and have a great time in life, however they want to live it.

5. Try to find peace. Our ultimate wish is to find peace in temple, in church, with Buddha, with shrinks, with drinks, with family, in our bodies, in our head, and in our hearts.

The Blip in the Road

As we grow older, the driving is not as smooth as it once was. There are blips along the road, and we just have to get past them. It's a little harder, but once we have done it, it's smooth sailing until the next one.

There are all kinds of blips. Little ones, like sprained wrists and ankles, which mean you can't play tennis for a couple of weeks. Medium ones, like knee or hip replacements, which mean you're out of commission for a couple of months. And big ones, like something with the heart or the diagnosis of a disease, which mean it might be a while before we get back in the game.

But they are all blips, just the same. We can and will drive right over them eventually. We have to look at the big picture, at the future. The key is to look ahead and remember we are all in it together! We can do this!

Drive on through, friends. Drive on through…

Accept, Adjust, and Move On

Maybe now that no one is looking, my looks won't be so important to me. That's a huge statement, coming from me. I grew up with a father who said, "Go put on your makeup. Company is coming." I was twelve.

"Why aren't my girls beauty-contest winners?" he asked. He made us feel our looks were the most important part of us. That was our currency, our worth. I got the message. I rebelled at first but eventually bought into it. Once in, I was caught in the web. I spent a great deal of my life making myself camera ready. I could have been doing something that would have made me grow as a person or would have helped others, but no, that was yet to come.

My sister Eileen died with her makeup purse next to her on the bed. Some of her last words to me were, "Am I still pretty?" She was, by the way. Amazing what conditioning can do. Still, if I left my makeup off, would I be sad to let that part of me go or just feel the relief? I don't know.

I do know one thing: To grow older means one has to accept, adjust, and move on!

There are so many things one has to accept. We have to dig deeper for meaning. So many things that we counted on are taken away: eyes, ears, feet. All of a sudden we can't see so well, our television sets are laughingly loud, and our feet can't wear our favorite stilettos. For sure, I used to laugh at those old ladies in comfortable shoes, but I get it now.

Even so, at night, when I go out with my husband

on a date, I put on my high heels and my makeup, and I like the way he and I feel about us. Plus I feel good about myself. So what am I even saying?

It's all very confusing! Perhaps some meaning will be revealed in the end.

Goodbye Mr. Chips

There was a movie that won actor Robert Donat an academy award in 1939. My mother or sisters must have taken me to see it. I was five years old at the time, but somehow it made a very strong impression on me. I don't know if I saw it years later when I was older or if I remember it from that year. The story was about an older professor and how much he influenced his young students. Toward the end, I think he was sick—I'm not sure about that part—and the students came to visit him because he was retiring. He was stooped over, in a gray wig, all made up with lots of wrinkles.

During the last thirty years, since I have lived here in Santa Barbara, I have had many young people help me, from transcribing my writings to painting on ceramics. They have been friends and daughters of friends or from various universities in the area.

I have cared for all of them. And when it was time for them to fly, I gave them my blessings, sometimes begrudgingly because they had been so helpful. Yet I had to let them go out in the world to do their thing. They would tell me about their boyfriends and girlfriends, and we would discuss their future.

Almost all of these young people have stayed in touch in one way or another, and I love hearing from them and being told what they have done in the last few years. One of my earliest assistants is now married and has a couple of children. She sends me photos from time to time.

The other day I received an email from a young man who had been an intern from UCSB. He had helped with the short documentary we made in 2011, *Stage IV, Living with Cancer.* He lives out of town and was here to see his sister, and I wondered what he wanted to say to me. I thought he might have wanted a reference for a job. My husband and I invited him to lunch. As it turned out, the young man just wanted to stop by and say hello.

He also wanted to tell us that working on the film had been a wonderful experience for him. I was touched that he would take the time to come and say that to me. So many people worked for nothing on that film and gave their time to help others. I felt it was a wonderful experience for those of us involved and was so glad he did, too.

I realized then that one of the benefits and opportunities of growing older is that we all get to be Mr. Chips in one way or another. We are able to help young people just by sharing our experiences with them, and they are eager to soak it up. It's a wonderful win-win for all involved.

The Rabbit Hole

If you asked me to come up with one word for this stage of aging, I would say "freefall." I feel like I am falling ever so gently down, down, down, toward the rabbit hole, just like Alice. I picture myself tumbling over and over in slow motion. It's not an entirely bad feeling. Sometimes it's quite pleasant. But it's different and therefore a little scary. There's so little structure in my life. Do you remember those emails that circulated years ago that said, "If I want to wear purple and read all night and sleep all day, who cares"? Well, that's kind of what it's like. I don't have to be anywhere at a certain time because I have unstructured myself on purpose. Still, it's odd. I am untethered.

The good news: If we want to go to the movies at 3 p.m. on a Tuesday, we can. If I want to take a nap in the middle of the day, I do. If I want to write my blog at midnight, I do that, too. I always find time to exercise in one way or another. Walks on the beach are a must! I'm concentrating on my photography, speaking, and writing. All in all, I am productive, but in a timeless freefall way. No schedules curtail me.

My housekeeper comes every Tuesday and Friday, as she has for twenty-five years. That's my benchmark for the days of the week. The rest of the week may be filled with a trip to the doctor, meetings, a meditation class, the gym, or lunch or dinner with friends. Is this the normal course of events for aging, or am I leading a very strange life, or both? I like it, and any pressure I feel is self-imposed, so I guess it really doesn't matter.

It seems I can wear purple and sleep all day if I want in my new freefall life and still get everything done in my own time.

What would Alice say?

2
Cancer Diagnosis

I T STARTED IN 2002. My husband and I were on vacation, and I had stomach pains. They weren't bad—just little sharp, jabbing pains. We decided I would see Dr. Kurt Ransohoff, our internist, when we returned home.

And so I did. The doctor told me to lie down, and he pressed my stomach. It hurt! He said, "Let's take an x-ray, Beverlye." And that was when he discovered the mass. Even though I had had a diagnosis of uterine lining cancer twelve years before, as far as I was concerned, I already had my cancer, and it was over. No one could live healthier than I did. I ate right, exercised, and felt I was doing everything I could for my health.

Though cancer ran rampant in my family—I had lost my grandmother, mother, and two sisters to the disease—it never entered my mind that these pains could mean anything. After many tests, another doctor in Los Angeles told me that I had eight tumors in the lining of my abdomen. That was on a Friday. He wanted me to go back into the hospital on Monday and start four kinds of chemotherapy, twenty-four hours a day, for three weeks. He said I would get very ill, and after I recovered he wanted to operate (assuming the tumors had shrunk). Once I had recovered from that operation, he wanted me to have the same chemo treatment again.

This didn't sound like a good idea to me at sixty-eight, not at that stage of my life! I wasn't sure my body could take it.

"I want another opinion," I said. However, three more doctors agreed with him. They all told me, "You have two months to live, Beverlye." Even so, my team (my husband, children, and their mates) lined up two more appointments for me. One was with Dr. Charles Forscher at Cedars-Sinai in Los Angeles and the other was with Dr. Frederick Eilber at UCLA. They were both heads of the sarcoma departments at their respective hospitals, and sarcoma was my type of cancer.

Dr. Forscher was the first doctor to look back at my earlier cancer cells and observe that they had traveled from my uterus into my abdomen and thus created the eight tumors. This was good news: It meant that because the tumors were hormone driven, I was open to hormone therapy. Dr. Forscher told me, "Go see Dr. Eilber; we are working together on this case, and we will come up with a treatment for you."

Of course, I'm leaving out all the sadness that went on during this period of my life. I had decided that if Dr. Eilber and Dr. Forscher couldn't come up with something beyond what the other doctors had prescribed, I would take a little light chemo to prolong living for a few months, and that was all. At this point my diagnosis was a fourth-stage, metastasized, inoperable, uteral stromal sarcoma.

But the doctors did have an idea. "We have come up with an experimental treatment for you," they told me. "It is a shot of Lupron and a pill of Femara... both are hormone blockers. We have to go before the tumor board for permission."

It made sense to me. I had a hormone-driven cancer, and these were going to block its growth if it worked.

"If you can get it passed," I told him, "I'll try it!" The doctors went before the tumor board, and three days later it was approved! I am still on that treatment many years later. My tumors are being starved and have remained 25 percent smaller. I did not realize how lucky I was to be at the very beginning of personalized medicine, target therapy, and hormone therapy—all new at that time. Only recently has this treatment been considered "not experimental" and given out to patients with hormone-driven cancers.

What Did I Learn?
1. Get more than one opinion.
Very important!
2. Form a team (relatives, friends, whoever).
3. Be your own advocate! You know your body. Listen to it! Then tell your doctor.
4. Become co-captain with your doctor.
5. Your doctor has hundreds of patients; you only have one.

6. Tell your friends and let them help. It makes them and you feel better.

7. Look to your cancer treatment center for all the wonderful, free classes they offer.

8. Do something creative to express your feelings.

9. Tell everyone you love how much they mean to you.

10. Pay it forward. Take everything you have learned, and pass it on to the next person diagnosed.

Novelist O.R. Melling says, "When you come to the edge of all that you know, you must believe one of two things: either there will be ground on which to stand, or you will be given wings to fly."

I was given wings to fly.

3
Hidden Thoughts

It's dark inside my head.
Cat scan to cat scan,
this temporary life I lead,
demons crawling round,
bumping into loneliness.
I begin to disconnect,
then feel a distance that makes me lonelier.
The black hole of
despondency always lurking.
Acting for others,
I put up a front.
Moments of hilarity,
seconds of fulfillment,
cat scan to cat scan,
hard on loved ones,
harder on myself.
These thoughts slip out, and so I hide them
behind a shield of a happy face.

4
My Family

MY PARENTS AND SISTERS are all gone now. Of course they would be. I was the baby, and I'm not a baby any longer.

Beverlye with her mother.

I was born in Seattle, Washington. My mother, Mae, and father, Bert, already had two older daughters, Thelma, thirteen, and Eileen, almost six. I was the baby of the three girls—the little one, they called me, or, sometimes, the rebel. My family wandered, and I wandered with them: from Spokane and a mink ranch to Portland, and then to California, where they and I stayed forever.

We lived in Studio City for a short time until we got our bearings, and my father got a profession. He became a developer. That sounded good. Sometimes it was fabulous, and sometimes it wasn't. I could never figure out if we had money or not. But it didn't seem to matter because we always lived like we did. My father would fix up houses and sell them, and we moved around a tremendous amount within the Los Angeles perimeter. That was hard for keeping friends but good for learning how to make new ones.

When we were little, we rode our bikes to our friends' houses, played jacks and hopscotch, and then rode home before dark. No one was worried. We were in the neighborhood, that's all. During these years aunts, cousins, and uncles came to live with us, or sometimes we went to live with them. I remember at five years old I went with my eleven-year-old sister across the country to stay with an aunt. That's how it was then. We were left alone or sent to live with relatives; no one helped with homework or applications for colleges. Needless to say, it was a different world.

We also lived through World War II. Fathers and brothers left and returned as heroes after fighting for our country. For the war effort, we kids collected tinfoil, newspapers, and rubber bands and did without butter and meat. We went through fake air raids and turned off our lights early, as we were told. We collected Green Stamps and sang patriotic songs. Our mothers and sisters made food for our soldiers and took it to the Stage Door Canteen. We wrote V-mails on funny onionskin paper. They were a letter and an envelope all in one and went overseas in a flash.

When the war ended in Europe, my family and I were living in Hollywood, and my sister Eileen and all her friends, my father and mother, sister Thelma (with her baby), and my friends all did a conga line down Hollywood Boulevard with me riding on the shoulders of one of my sisters' boyfriends. I had the perfect seat. It was a grand, celebratory day I'll never forget. The soldiers, including my brother-in-law—who hadn't seen his baby yet—would be coming home. We loved America. We had won the war. Everything was going to be like it was before.

After that, when I was fourteen, the family finally landed in Beverly Wood, on the west side of Los Angeles, and occupied one of three new houses my Dad had built. There were bean fields all around us. We had street parties on the weekends, with car doors open, music blaring, and all of us dancing.

Mama Mae

My mother was zestful and glamorous in her knit suits with matching turbans. A voluptuous, slim-legged, wonderful-smelling woman packed into a five-foot frame! She was Mama Mae to her friends, Mother to her three daughters, and Nana to her grandchildren. She died when she was sixty-three, of colon cancer, after being terribly ill for two years. Cancer was kept as a dirty secret in those days. Even the word wasn't said out loud. She followed in the footsteps of her mother, who had died at the same age.

Mae Fisher—mother.

I was twenty-nine, and she was a mystery to me. Maybe because I was a rebel, she decided wisely to leave me for my sisters to raise. I wish I had made the effort to know her better. Maybe she was just tired of parenting responsibilities by the time I was born. She loved her daughters, her sisters, her grandchildren, and her man, that I know for sure. I hope she knew I loved her, too. The tender side of me came from my Mom.

Some of These Days

My mother sang at parties,
not opera or Cole Porter,
mind you.
This five-foot woman
had a couple of drinks and belted,
"Some of these days, I'm gonna miss you honey."
It embarrassed me then.
I love the thought of it now.
Was that Sophie Tuckeresque person
always
buried inside that two-piece knit?
How I wish I could tell her
I'm no longer embarrassed.
Now I would jump up right alongside her,
look into her face,
and sing,
"I'm gonna miss you honey."

My Father

If I had to use only one word to describe my father,
Bert, it would be "exciting." There are many other
ways I could go with this word game: unpredictable,
tasteful, unreasonable, smart, charming, distant, fun,
generous, and glamorous. He was all of these things.
I guess that's what made him exciting! I didn't say
easy; I said exciting! He lavished gifts on us, but he
wasn't around much. It was a tradeoff. He was a self-
taught man. He would read up about antiques and

rugs and jewelry and go to auctions and bring home unbelievable treasures and set them out on the dining room table. He decorated all our houses in beautiful taste. He was the son of an Orthodox rabbi who came over on the boat when he was nine. How did he get interested in décor and antiques? I wish I could call and ask him!

Bert Fisher—father.

Bert was quite handsome and rumored to be a ladies' man, but he was unbelievably devoted to my mother after she became ill and until she died. They

43

had a stormy but loving marriage. They would argue, and then, later, when he took a nap on the couch, she would come over and tenderly cover him. Mae died in his arms at home, with all her girls around her.

"I meant to be another Conrad Hilton," he whispered to me as he lay dying. I didn't ever remember him confiding in me before. I was shocked! He had disappointed himself, and I hadn't realized that. I had always thought he was very successful, but more importantly, I thought he felt that about himself. He died at seventy-five in the hospital after his last heart attack. We were all there.

Any artistic talent I have came from my Dad. Now that I think about it, the decorating and moving sound familiar, too.

Maybe I'm aging in high heels because of him. He always wanted his girls to be glamorous and wear them. I still hear you, Dad, loud and clear!

The Sisterhood

When Nora Ephron died, I grieved for many reasons. First of all, she was an amazing talent, and I never wanted to see that quelled. I still wanted so much more from her. She told us how hideous divorce was but how there could still be a happy ending. She told us all how she hated her neck and how to laugh at ourselves as we aged. I loved how she wrote! And, yes, she had three sisters. I keep thinking about them. I could easily relate to how they felt.

The Fisher girls—Eileen, Beverlye, and Thelma.

I also lost my sisters. When I heard that Nora's sister Delia had written a book, I couldn't wait to order it. I wanted to hear how she expressed her thoughts about her sister. I needed to hear how someone else could put into words what it meant to lose her. Of course, Delia did a wonderful job. She's an eloquent writer. It brought up all my old feelings but in a good way. She made me want to write about what it's like to be part of the "sisterhood."

I wanted to write about how wonderful my sisters were to me, and about how much fun we had, and, yes, about how much I miss them. I would love to turn around to them and say, "Remember when

Mother did that?"

My eldest sister, Thelma, was part mother, part sister to me, and I lived with her at times. Eileen was my best friend and idol. She took me everywhere with her. I went with her the first day she started college at the University of Southern California. She let me sleep in her room at night when I needed to talk, and she let me wear her cashmere sweaters to school when I started Beverly Hills High School. (Like the Ephron girls, I, too, went to BHHS.) I was fifteen years old when Eileen got married and left home. I was devastated! I slept over at her honeymoon apartment all the time. She even taught me how to cook.

When I got married, she made me a detailed list for my first dinner. "Heat the oven," she wrote. "Put the brisket, surrounded by carrots and onions and potatoes, in the oven and cover with water. Now go take a shower, and apply your makeup, and comb your hair. Come back, set the table, and put pretty flowers in the middle. Now put the string beans, with onion soup, on top, in the oven. It's time to make a salad. Combine lettuce with peas (frozen and thawed) and Girard's Dressing. Just before dinner, light the candles, and you're ready." That was my sister Eileen; she did everything to perfection.

Thelma was beautiful. She married a handsome man and had three gorgeous children. I was six years old when she got married and moved out. I hated that she left. She and her husband, Vic, were so obviously in love! They were wonderful to me. I adored them and their kids. They took time to help with my homework. They taught me how to horseback ride, and they listened to me. My parents were fun but not big on any of that.

But the most fun the three of us sisters had together was dancing! There was always Latin music playing, and we loved to dance. (Of course they had taught me.)

I no longer cry when I think of my sisters—well, maybe once in a while—but what I do instead is see sweet pictures of them in my head: We are dancing or fishing on my Dad's boat. Thelma is eating a liverwurst sandwich in the kitchen, loving it. Eileen and I are pregnant together, comparing bellies. My Mom and Dad and we three sisters and our husbands are playing cards on a Tuesday night at the house on Cresta Drive. Everyone is laughing, eating, and peeking at each other's cards. That's what we did!

I only have happy thoughts when I think of my sisters, now. I no longer picture them being ill.

Hang in, Delia.

Last Man Standing

I loved the guy Thelma married. Victor Selten was the handsomest man I had ever seen! He had dark wavy hair, dimples, and a build like Hercules. He and Thelma were crazy about each other. I can picture them vividly, dancing in our cozy den to "Besame Mucho." They were wonderful dancers.

One of my greatest memories, when I was about ten, was Vic coming to my school to surprise me.

He was in the armed services and was working on the atom bomb (though we did not know that at the time). His whereabouts were secret. He was not allowed to come home. He even missed the birth of his first-born son. Eventually, though, he came home on leave, and as I looked out the window of my classroom, there he was, so handsome in his uniform, with his hat perched on his head at a perfect angle. The teacher let him come in, and I ran into his arms.

As I grew up, my brother-in-law became an idol to me. Vic was kind, sweet, and patient. When I was twelve years old, and my parents were finishing our latest house, I went to live with him, Thelma, and their three children in San Diego for six months. I loved living there, even though I missed my parents and it was a hard time in my life. The house was filled with children and laughter and, of course, Latin music, because it was part of the culture at that time! Vic would help me with my homework every night. He also took me to the stables every Saturday for riding lessons. After the semester was over, I moved back to Los Angeles, and when my girlfriends from Beverly Hills High met Vic, they developed huge crushes on him, too.

Sadly, my sister passed away when she was fifty-five years old from ovarian cancer. Vic never married again, but he did have a lovely lady in his life during his last fifteen years, and they went dancing every Friday night. Vic was fortunate enough to live to see grandchildren and great-grandchildren. He passed away three months short of his ninety-fifth birthday, leaving me to be the last man standing—the eldest of that generation in my family.

We remained close throughout our lives, and I will miss him terribly, but somewhere, far away, I can hear the strains of Pérez Prado playing, and I can picture my sister and Vic dancing and looking into each other's eyes!

They are back together at last.

I hope their song never ends!

5
Letting Go

ALL OF US, as time goes on, have trouble letting go of memories, conversations, and circumstances. My husband says I keep conversations in a vault and bring them back when I need to. It's true, I admit it. Slowly but surely, I'm trying to put a lock on that vault.

Letting Go

Some things we can change.
Others, we cannot.
Sometimes we can fix situations,
come in a side door, and surprise our destiny,
but most days we just have to let go.
Maybe that's our lesson this time around.
We can live with this or that if we have to.
It's a trade-off.
Living a life of unfulfilled expectations,
or simply letting go.
Easy.

The Unexpected Guest

How do you deal with the uninvited? How should we handle something or someone—thoughts or actions or people—that just drops in? Unexpected good news and unexpected bad news both shake up our world. Sometimes we come up with plan B easily and immediately. Sometimes we just stay stuck. Either way, it's a lesson.

A while ago, my husband and I both had bad colds and were in and out of bed for two weeks. My first day out, the sun was shining, and I couldn't wait to take a walk with a friend. When we came back to her house, there was a big dog in the street. Worried that he would be run over, I told my friend I was going to buzz her neighbor to come get him. Suddenly the dog ran down the street, leapt up, and fiercely bit my arm. (No good deed goes unpunished!) A visit to urgent care followed—no stitches or tetanus shot, just cleaning, antibiotics, and butterfly bandages—but I realized that there was a lesson in that uninvited dog bite: Pay attention and take care of yourself first… and then take care of everyone and everything else.

Sometime the surprises work out better. My single cousin (five years younger than me) was minding her own business at a bridge tournament, when an unexpected guest sat down next to her. By the end of the week they were in love. She had planned out the rest of her days with children and grandchildren and bridge and business matters, but here was love, right in front of her, and she went for it. I later met her "new best friend," and he seemed charming and absolutely goofy about her. Both of their smiles were absolutely blinding.

Joseph Campbell wrote, "We must be willing to get rid of the life we planned, so as to have the life that is waiting for us." So there you have it. Step out of the way, folks, and let the unexpected in!

Friendly Ghosts

After I gave a talk for the American Cancer Society's 100th anniversary in Santa Barbara, we went to the Desert (as it's called these days) for a few days to relax. Friends of ours had offered my husband and me their house. They said, "You can bring Sophia!" An invitation for my dog? That did it. Bob, Sophia, and I lying in the sun with nothing to do sounded wonderful to me. We arrived at this lovely 1970s Steven Chase–designed house, and it was just what the doctor ordered! It had a view of the mountains and golf course with a charming pool. Perfect!

Is it just me, or as we age do our memories and our ghosts go with us wherever we go? They may be friendly ghosts, mind you, but they're ghosts, nevertheless. The Desert was our place in the Fifties, Sixties, and Seventies. It was called Palm Springs then, and we went with our families over the holidays as kids, with our friends over spring breaks as teenagers, and with our husbands and children as young marrieds. We danced at the Chi Chi club, dined at Don the Beachcomber and Las Casuelas Terraza, and burned ourselves to a crisp at the Hotel Del Tahquitz pool.

Everywhere I looked on this trip, I saw friendly ghosts. There I was in an off-the-shoulder blouse wearing capris, a short Gene Shacove (hairdresser to the stars!) haircut, and big hoop earrings, thinking I looked a little bit like Gina Lollobrigida.

I saw my mother and father (more friendly ghosts) staying at the brand new Ocotillo Lodge, having the time of their lives. My sisters and their families were all there, too. Our kids were splashing in the pool. Everyone was young, healthy, and happy to be together.

The next friendly ghosts were my young husband and children at Charlie Farrells's Racquet Club. What a glamorous place that was! Everyone in show business was there. My kids took tennis lessons from Roxie alongside Kirk Douglas and a bunch of celebrity offspring. We had breakfasts at Louise's Pantry. For Christmas we rented houses with velvet-covered couches and basketball hoops in the front yard. We brought our favorite music with us, and listened to Tony Bennett singing "I want to be around to pick up the pieces."

There were sad ghosts, too. I remember sitting in the bathtub with tears rolling down my cheeks because my mother was dying.

I continue to love the Desert. I had a birthday weekend for Bob there years ago and have brought my children and my grandchildren there. Our favorite thing to do was to take a walk on the main street, get an ice cream, and go into the bookstore.

Of course, it's changed now. The Desert has turned into Rancho Mirage, Palm Desert, La Quinta, Cathedral City, and a myriad of other towns, but I'm still partial to Palm Springs, because that's where my memories are. On this last trip Bob and I had a wonderful time. We rested in that beautiful home, saw friends, and took long walks. It was great to see everyone from the past, real and remembered, and, of course, we had an ice cream and walked down the main street.

6
What We Do for Love

MY HUSBAND AND I have been together for more than thirty years—in our own way, however. Up until a couple of years ago we had not really lived together. We had a house in Santa Barbara, and a condo in Los Angeles. Bob worked during the week, and he would come up to Santa Barbara on Thursday afternoons. Sometimes I would go down for a day or two. I loved going down, seeing family or having dinner with friends, but many weeks I was too busy with commitments. My daily life was in Santa Barbara. When I was home alone, sometimes I would have poached eggs for dinner, or even cereal. I loved it.

When my husband came up on Thursday, it was like dating. We would both be excited to see each other. I would get dressed and put on makeup. I would have a special dinner waiting for him, or we'd have plans to eat with friends, but our weekends were reserved for each other. Bob would play golf, and I would hike, but we took special care with each other's feelings. Then, over time, everything changed!

Bob retired, we rented out the condo in Los Angeles, and moved to Santa Barbara full time. OMG! Be careful what you wish for. We couldn't figure out what day it was, because weekends were now the same as weekdays. Golf no longer had the same appeal, now that Bob could do it every day. Meanwhile, I was totally bewildered. Should I go out, as he encouraged me to do, for lunches and dinners with girlfriends? Cook real breakfasts, lunches, and dinners every day?

Beverlye and Bob on their wedding day.

My routines came to a halt. I liked to exercise upon rising and then eat; Bob liked to eat breakfast and exercise afterward. I gave him my little studio to use as an office, so he worked in his office, and I worked in mine. He went to sleep early and woke up at 6 a.m. I watched TV and read far into the night and then woke in the middle of the night and read some more. I slept late. We got on each other's nerves!

Well, guess what? I discovered that I liked my husband to be working down the hall, and that I could say, "I have to go to the post office, want to grab a bite to eat afterward?" That's our new version of Thursday dates. We each have our own errands and then meet for lunch...or not. Every day is different, but we have found our rhythm. Bob even likes playing golf again. Once in a while he surprises me with, "Let's have poached eggs or cereal for dinner tonight."

He still spends a little time working in the music business and goes to L.A. for meetings. Maybe he'll do more, and maybe he won't. Meanwhile, he's begun to get used to me taking photos, writing blogs, and having people who help me with my endeavors come and go in the house. He's got ideas, I've got ideas, and we're both willing to listen.

What's wrong with this picture? Nothing! It's just what we do for love!

The Roller Coaster

Life has its ups and downs, just like a roller coaster. I went to a wonderful sixtieth-anniversary celebration recently for a longtime friend. In the midst of all the joy someone whispered in my ear that another friend's husband—someone we had all known since high school—had just passed away. So here we were at a celebration, discussing a funeral. The more I think about it, however, a funeral is a celebration too, but one that involves a heavy heart, as well as a feeling of letting go of emotions.

Sebastian Cole has written, "With peaks of joy and valleys of heartache, life is a roller coaster ride, the rise and fall of which defines our journey. It is both scary and exciting at the same time."

At this time of our lives, we are just going to have to accept, adjust, and move on, as those we love go on ahead. It is our friends, after all, who weave the tapestry of our lives; to lose thread after thread is to watch the tapestry unravel.

I no longer want to play musical chairs to see who didn't get a chair when the music stops.

Funerals Make Me Hungry

As we grow older,
we all live in the midst of a minefield.
We have to be careful where we step.
To the right and to the left is certain peril.
Another friend dropped out of our life today
like a plane from the sky.
We gathered to extol his virtues, then we ate,
always filling up that hole,
hungry for life not lived.
No turkey, coleslaw, bagel, or cake can fill up
that hole,
nor replace the life, that to us,
was cut impossibly short.

Kindness Karma

The day started out with my husband catching an early plane to New York. We were in Los Angeles at the time. And I remember Bob kissing me on the cheek and saying, "I love you." I murmured, "Have a good flight; I love you, too," and went right back to sleep. I woke up a couple of hours later, and when I went to brush my teeth I noticed Bob had left his cell phone in the bathroom.

"Damn," I thought. He's on a business trip, and he'll need it. I walked to the FedEx office, bought a box and packing slip, came back home, put the phone in the box, then went back to FedEx and mailed it. Bob would have it early the next morning. Later he called me, and as he started frantically to tell me he'd forgotten his phone, I broke in and said, "I already sent it." He was thrilled.

The same day, while I was still feeling good about doing something helpful for my husband, the most extraordinary thing happened. I was in a new doctor's office, and a nurse asked me for my insurance card. I reached into my purse and realized that I had changed purses and forgotten to put my wallet back in. Not only did I not have my insurance card, but I also didn't have a driver's license, a credit card, or any cash to get out of the parking garage! Since I'd never been to this doctor before, I didn't want to ask anyone if I could borrow some money.

Then I remembered that Dr. Forscher, my oncologist, had an office down the street somewhere. I called his nurse and asked if she would loan me twenty dollars; I would send her a check the next day. But while we were on the phone, I felt a hand on my shoulder, and I heard another patient say, "Don't put yourself though all that. I'll give you twenty-five dollars, just in case you need another five."

"You don't even know me," I said. "How do you know you'll be paid back"? I don't remember the rest of our exchange, but I do remember she went through the trouble of changing some money to make sure she had the right amount for me. She gave me a card and said, "Just send me a check. This could happen to anyone. Don't worry about it." I went home smiling. A small incident like that reminded me there are still trusting people in the world. It renewed my faith in humanity.

Kindness karma! Pass it on!

7
Chapters of Our Lives

REMEMBERING IS AS MUCH a part of aging as forgetting. I remember events, sentences, and stories from the Forties and Fifties as if they were taking place at this moment. Words from old songs pop up in my head, and I sing them, without even noticing that I know all the words. When I am awake in the middle of the night, these images and sounds float around like old friends who have come to visit.

I grew up in Beverly Hills in the Forties before Gucci, Armani, and Bijan ever thought of coming there. Rodeo Drive was just the location of our bike shop (Hans Ort), our dry cleaner (Filoy), and market (Jergensen's), and, of course, of our saddle and blue jeans store, Mayfair Riding Shop. We went to Blum's for cake, Wil Wright's for ice cream, Ah Fong's for Chinese food, and the Luau for a big date night.

Walking into the Luau was entering another world. Handsome Joe was the maitre d', and Louie, the friendly waiter, waited on us from the time we were dating to years later when I was married and had children. The Luau's owner was Steve Crane, an ex-husband of Lana Turner's, and because of that, there was always someone glamorous at every table.

We grew up alongside movie stars and about-to-become movie stars, and they were all simply a part of the patchwork of our lives. Richard Chamberlain was just a nice boy in my English class. Those of us from Beverly Hills High went to Bisbee's, Simon's, and Dolores Drive-In, so we could sneak a peek at the tough guys from Los Angeles and Fairfax High. We had school dances in the swim gym right after we had watched a swim meet on the famous floor that opened. Because of that famous floor, an oil well, and a parking lot, our school was always in the news. There was no Century City in our landscape yet, just the charming little town of Beverly Hills next to the equally charming town of Westwood. (When I think of Westwood, the first thing that comes to mind is a great ham and cheese sandwich at the Chatham restaurant for lunch.)

As for other favorite spots, let's not forget the Brown Derby for a great salad and Hunter's Bookstore for our favorite book. We went to Ye Little Club to hear singers and the Bantam Cock to hear music. After dates, we hung out at MFK's (Milton F. Kreis's) to discuss the night.

We would go to the Brazilian Room to rumba and cha-cha to a great Latin beat, then end up at the Ready Room to listen to Matt Dennis. Sometimes we'd catch the late show at Billy Gray's Band Box. There was no traffic, just diagonal parking and no parking meters. These were simple times, safe times, and, most of all, fun times, and how delicious and uncomplicated they were!

Beverlye in the early 1970s.

After graduation from high school, I went to the University of California at Los Angeles (UCLA). As was the case in most households of that era, my parents' biggest interest was in my getting married as quickly as possible. I had already met my future husband at seventeen, much to their delight, so at the very mature age of nineteen, I married a USC man who was twenty-one. I dropped out of UCLA pronto and, within three months, found myself happily pregnant. I had both my children—a girl and a

63

boy—by the time I was twenty-three. That's what we did in those days.

The interesting thing about growing up in Beverly Hills in that generation is that people didn't move away. They got married and stayed friends with their schoolmates forever. Their children also went to Beverly Hills schools, and they all became friends with each other. And so it went. My kids went to El Rodeo and Beverly Hills High, and they had some of the same teachers I had. We still went to the Luau for dinner and Ah Fong's on Sunday night. The Mayfair Riding Shop leased to Gucci early on, and most of the other restaurants of our youth disappeared. We still meet at La Scala for our favorite salad, however, or go to Nate and Al's for a turkey sandwich on corn rye. But Beverly Hills is not our same old sleepy town anymore. The world has discovered Rodeo Drive.

As much as I adore Santa Barbara—and I do—I left a piece of my heart in Beverly Hills…the Beverly Hills before Gucci that is!

The Paths We Have Chosen

One of the benefits of growing older is that I can look back and see where I consciously or unconsciously turned left instead of right. I think about women and events that not only changed my life but also put me on the path to where I am today. For better or worse, I made my choices.

In the Sixties I was at a dinner party, and a woman I didn't know said, "Does anyone want to share an art studio with me in Venice?"

"I do," I said quickly, much to my then-husband's surprise. For fifteen years I had been painting in a little room between my two children's bedrooms. I was excited beyond belief at the thought of having a real art studio and being with other artists.

The studio was owned by a famous needlepoint designer who taught in Beverly Hills. Smart and charismatic, she was a tall, dramatic-looking woman who wore long dresses, beads, and turbans. After her husband died, she sold everything and bought a church in Venice, California, and called it St. Jives by the Sea. She lived in the front, stained-glass windows and all, and rented out the back of the church to artists.

So I moved my artwork into this gloriously large studio, and not only did I fall in love with Venice, but it changed my path forever. I met women who were painters, writers, and sculptors; they all earned money for what they loved to do! What a feeling of power and self-worth that must have given them. They designed their own lives, and I wanted that, too. The atmosphere at St. Jives was joyful, with lots of cooking, guitar playing, and exchanging of ideas. It made me feel alive.

Venice was emerging as the West Coast version of Greenwich Village in New York. Laddie Dill, Robert Graham, and DeWain Valentine were just a few of the artists who lived and painted there. Venice was booming. I was in the middle of it, and I was enthralled!

On television, Betty Friedan and Gloria Steinem were talking about equal pay and equal rights for women. I read Marilyn French's book *The Women's Room* and Germaine Greer's *The Female Eunuch*. My thoughts and desires were changing. The road that lay ahead was scary, but there was no turning back.

I sold a couple of paintings to the actress Suzanne Pleshette, who was a friend of mine, and she suggested it was time for me to have a show. I had my first exhibit at a place called The Staircase in Beverly Hills. To my amazement, people actually bought my paintings, and I, too, was making money for what I loved to do. I had many shows after that, and eventually did design a new life for myself filled with adventure and creativity.

I think of those women often, with gratitude for putting me on the road less traveled.

Memories

One recent morning, after I had slept over at my daughter's house, she brought me some rice cereal in a bowl I had designed in Italy. As I looked at that bowl I remembered a fantastic chapter of my life.

I had been painting in St. Jives by the Sea for many years, but the studio eventually had to be sold, and I needed another place to paint. I found the perfect space above an upholstery store on Melrose Avenue, down the street from the famous, star-studded restaurant Ma Maison. I stayed in that studio until 1984 and, after my divorce, bought a small house on beautiful grounds in Montecito and built the art studio of my dreams. I was going with Bob then, and I became interested in the ceramics business. For about two years I designed ceramics with a Peruvian company. Unfortunately, that firm took all the money we earned and evaporated, leaving me in the lurch. I was devastated!

One day someone told me about a ceramics factory in Deruta—a small town between Florence and Rome—that brought in guest artists who would design and sell their goods in the Italian showroom. One had to be accepted by Ubaldo Grazia, the owner of the magnificent old *fabbrica*. Bob and I took a bunch of photos of my dishes, went to Europe, and called on Signor Grazia. He took me on, and I went to Deruta alone to make a line of dishes. It sounds easier than it was, but I was up for the adventure, one of the most exciting times of my life. I stayed at a farmhouse run by an Italian couple. It was an *agriturismo*—the papa raised the food and the grapes, and the mamma cooked the meals.

I walked to the factory and for six to eight hours a day designed alongside the Italian painters, then walked home to my tiny room in the farmhouse. I was excited and lonely at the same time. No one spoke English except Signor Grazia and one other artist, and for a long time only painfully bad Italian would come out of my mouth.

This went on for four years, for three weeks at a time. My Italian got better, though, and I became more familiar with the area. Bob would meet me at the end of the three weeks, and we would travel through Italy together. Our love was blooming. It was a glorious time.

Surrounded by her designs in Deruta, Italy.

There was a lot of business and a lot of work attached to it. I brought home samples of the ceramics and sold them at shows at friend's homes, hotels, and restaurants. Meanwhile the orders kept coming, and I hired help and ran the business out of my new studio and garage. But there no time to paint, and my studio was always filled with people waiting for instructions.

A few decisions had to be made. Keep the business going? Hire more employees? Get a factory to house the inventory? Give up painting?

I decided to keep on painting and slowly went out of the ceramics business. I loved the quiet of my studio nestled in the trees in Montecito and wanted to keep it that way. One has to have lived a certain amount of years to gather different chapters of one's life. I smile whenever I think of the Italian chapter in mine.

The Passage of Time

I can't pretend that each birthday doesn't have my full attention. I love that I've lived to see my granddaughter driving and my grandsons becoming young men with low voices. My attitude is definitely one of gratitude. I know that's a cliché, but life is a cliché after all.

Where did time go? Did I blink too many times? In my mind's eye, I've just received my own driver's license and have come out of the front door to see that beautiful yellow-and-blue Ford Fairlane that my Dad bought for me. I must have blinked again. My babies, who a moment ago were crawling on the carpet in our Cheviot Hills home, are now baby boomers with teenagers of their own. I'm not watching their tennis matches and baseball games, we're watching *their* children's volleyball, baseball, and lacrosse games. Blink, blink, blink!

Bob and I are happy staying at home now, with the fire going, watching *The Voice* or *60 Minutes*. But wasn't that us, playing tennis all day, barhopping, and hitting the hot spots? I must have blinked once more. Who are those two older people in all the photographs? Have they hired actors to take our places? If so, why did they hire people with so many wrinkles?

The passage of time plays funny tricks on all of us. None of the sentences people say to me make sense anymore, because I don't hear the words correctly. We end up saying "What?" a lot in our house. Are we not paying attention? Or are we losing our hearing? I'm not sure I want to know the answer to that one.

We go to the gym, we exercise, we hike, but everything has shifted. As Gypsy Rose Lee said in her later years, "I still have all the same measurements, they're just lower." Tell it like it is, Gypsy!

The days go so fast now, but I still look for days full of meaning and joy. I find them in my marriage, in my family, in my dog, in the beach, in photography, in writing, and in giving back. Am I missing something? That's what worries me in this passage of time.

I will look in every nook and corner to find pure joy and contentment in these next ten years.

8

Ultimate Emotion

LYRICS OF SONGS mean so much to me now (and I don't mean Nicki Minaj's "Yassss Bish"). I weep whenever I hear Willie Nelson sing, "Always on My Mind," or Bruno Mars in "Just the Way You Are." I want to feel all kinds of emotion, hurt along with love. It's the time of life to dig deep.

Ultimate Emotion

I want to sit down and write a concerto that
will bring you to your knees.
I want to belt out blues that will
make your eyes well up to the brim.
I want to write a play where the third act
rings so true,
everyone stands and yells, "Bravo!"
I want to dance wildly on the beach
under a starry sky.
I want to run through the fields of Kenya,
with the giraffes bounding alongside me.
I want to climb the highest peak in Nepal
and yell out over the mountaintops,

"I made it!"
I want only to feel
the ultimate emotion.
After all is said and done
isn't that what we all want?

9
Maintenance

Dear Jane Fonda,
I know it must be glorious to be you,
even with your everyday problems.
There is something I need to discuss
with you, however.
I've been a fan of yours from early on.
You started an exercise regime; I exercised
with you.
You looked good; I looked good.
But Miss Fonda, Jane, really?
Prime Time in our seventies?
I don't think so!
These are not our salad years, Jane.
These are the dessert years of our lives.
We can still enjoy ourselves.
We can dance, and we can sing.
But, really, it's not the same as before,
is it?
I don't remember sleeplessness, dryness, leg
cramps, cataracts, backaches, and bleary eyes
in my thirties and forties.
So while I'm still your biggest fan,
just like you, I do everything I can

to keep my romance alive, my high heels on,
a smile on my face.
And as much as I loved your book, I have to
say:
Please forgive me for being crass,
but Prime Time my ass, Miss Fonda
Prime Time my ass.

Changing the Drapes

Let's discuss maintenance! I don't mean maintenance on your house or your car. I'm talking about our every day, every week, every month maintenance on ourselves. I'm saying it's a forever thing! I'm talking about hair color, teeth cleaning, Pilates, yoga, zumba, botox, fillers (just a little when necessary, no big lips), facials (just a cleansing and maybe a little scraping), manicures, pedicures, waxing, eyebrow shaping, chiropractor (for our neck or back), acupuncture, and on and on.

Once we turn fifty, it's a whole new ball game. It's like changing the drapes in the living room, and suddenly everything else in the room looks shabby. When you have your eyebrows done, shouldn't the rest of your face look as good? Of course! There has to be an entire new budget allotment for our after-fifty maintenance. And it's not cheap! I'm not discussing buying new clothes. Even if we shop in our own closet (which I love to do), there are still alterations. Maybe the styles are shorter now, or maybe we've gained or lost a few pounds. Shoes need to be soled, purses need to be fixed.

And by the way, maintenance is very time consuming! Every day we have to do something—a hike, a visit to the gym, or a swim, get our nails done, do something for our face. That's maintenance! It's a great (and unusual) week when everything has kicked in and we are looking good and feeling great. That means roots colored, nails and toes polished, and so on.

I say, let's be grateful for maintenance. That means we are alive and kicking and still wanting to look and feel our very best. It's actually a very small price to pay!

Shopping

I had lunch the other day with two friends, and we were all talking about aging (what else is new?), the surprises it has in store for us, and what makes us happy. One friend said that shopping still makes her happy. No matter how the day starts, she ends up thrilled if she shopped and scored. You score if you find something you like on sale (the bigger the sale, the bigger the score) or if you find the perfect tights or cocktail napkins in a funny little shop where you were just browsing. Even if something is not on sale, it may be just what you've been looking for. It's like the Eagles sing in "Heartache Tonight": "Everybody wants to take a little chance, make it come out right." Shopping is kind of like running. It gets your endorphins singing.

Shopping isn't quite what it used to be for us, however. Once, whatever you tried on looked great; now we just have to be a little creative. My motto is camouflage what you don't like and show off what you do!

One of my favorite things about shopping is the returning! You've bought something, brought it home, and found out you have two other things just like it. (That's what attracted you in the first place; it was familiar.) Now you get to feel virtuous by getting your money back. Not long ago in San Francisco, I saw a beautiful blue dress, and I thought how perfect that would be for winter with some black tights. Tried it on, and it fit very well. Bought it, brought it home, and there it was hanging in my closet—a blue wool dress that Bob had bought me a couple of months ago that I hadn't even worn yet. Luckily, I could return the second one.

And the best news is, I still have a blue dress!

The Reflection in the Mirror

We all have pictures of ourselves in our head. I'm always surprised when I see my reflection in a mirror or shop window. Is that really who I've become? The answer, of course, is yes! I had my years of wearing a blue strapless dress. I'm someone else now.

Maybe someone smarter, wiser, and more tolerant.

It's someone else's turn in the dress, and I'm fine with that...most of the time!

The Dress

In those days,
I slipped into my crinolines with my merry
widow on top,
and at the last moment stepped into my strapless blue dress.
Days spent basking in the sun, tan shoulders,
strong arms.
Fifty years later, those arms are in long sleeves.
The tan has faded long ago.
But the vision of me in the strapless dress,
will remain part of my image
in my mind's eye forever.

10
The Answer

"B UT WHAT I LIKE doing *best* is *nothing*," said Christopher Robin.

On a day when life is overwhelming, when everything and everyone is too much, when you feel like you can't hear any more bad news about anyone, when you can't make another decision, or look at your computer one more minute, you can climb into your comfy bed and pull the covers over your head and stay there for the rest of the day. To me, there is nothing more luxurious than a day in my own bed (when you are not sick, of course). It is better than a facial, a manicure, or a massage for two reasons:

1. You are alone and don't have to talk to anyone.
2. It's free.

Here are the requirements: Everyone must be out of the house, the door closed, curtains drawn. There should be good reading material on the bed within reach. Hopefully, delicious leftover food is in the refrigerator, fruit and nuts are available for grazing on a tray on the bed, and the TV is turned to an old movie where you can either cry or laugh—something like *Casablanca* or *The Hangover*. You can even watch dumb daytime TV shows. In fact, you can watch anything that requires no brain cells for as long as you like.

No phones should be answered. Cell phones and computers should be turned off or at least put in another room, so you don't hear that ping from a new message. Dozing is encouraged. Nothing constructive should be done. No thank-you notes written, no emails returned. Put cream on your face without observing new wrinkles. This is your renewal day!

I try to make time for this once a month. Computers need refreshing; don't we? I don't feel guilty about this pastime, nor should you. Keep it as a special day for yourself. I promise you will wake up the next day ready to tackle the world.

This is my answer to stress in our way-too-demanding life.

WARNING: If you start to do this once or twice a week, call your physician.

Being in the Moment

Walt Whitman wrote, "Not in another place… Not for another hour, but this hour." How powerful that is! After all, how many of us can appreciate this moment? So much of the time we are worried about tomorrow and the day after. Or we relive some event that happened yesterday, wishing it had turned out better. If our picnic had better weather… if our hike could have had more shade… if that restaurant had better service, then all of those moments would have been perfect.

If, if, if.

In fact, we ruined that particular moment by thinking, if only we could have made it perfect. Actually, it was perfect all along. And if we had been in that moment, we would have realized it.

My sister used to say, whenever I lamented my next birthday, "Enjoy today, because this is the youngest you will ever be." How true! I wish I could go back and talk to myself at forty so I could realize how young I was. I wish I hadn't wasted a minute thinking about it and just enjoyed the moment. That is true with many moments in our lives.

I want to grab hold of every moment and keep it close! I want to be more aware, not just about aging, but about everything that matters, "not in another place… not for another hour, but this hour."

A Fresh Start

In rereading *The Wise Heart* by Jack Kornfield, I always find something to reflect upon. Here is an excerpt: "In *High Tide in Tucson*, novelist Barbara Kingsolver talks about how this transformation is possible, even when our old life is in ruins:

'Every one of us is called upon, probably many times, to start a new life. A frightening diagnosis, a marriage, a move, loss of a job or a limb or a loved one, a graduation, bringing a new baby home: it's impossible to think at first how this all will be possible. Eventually, what moves it forward is the subterranean ebb and flow of being alive among the living.

'In my own worst seasons I've come back from the colorless world of despair by forcing myself to look hard, for a long time, at a single glorious thing: a flame of red geranium outside my bedroom window. And then another: my daughter in a yellow dress. And another: the perfect outline of a full, dark sphere behind the crescent moon. Until I learned to be in love with my life again. Like a stroke victim retraining new parts of the brain to grasp lost skills, I have taught myself joy, over and over again.'"

In my case I have had many starting-over situations. During my childhood I moved many times and continue to do so in my adult life. There was new life after divorce, a new city, new friends, new life after diagnosis, a new marriage.

We *are* able to change our story. We can teach ourselves to change our harmful thoughts from the past and believe in the possibility of tomorrow. As we age, we need to trust our true nature and believe in ourselves even more and to be constantly ready for a fresh start.

It is never too late.

Shameless Indulgence

Sometimes we need a little treat. Some days we need to be a little naughty and end up with a smile on our face. I think we have to be able to get away with something and not have to pay the piper. Just a *little* something.

We have to be good so much of the time. We eat

right, exercise, pay our bills, keep up our houses, love our families. We take care of our pets and keep our cars washed. Life demands so much from us, we can afford to have a little extra happiness. There are days when we need a little lift at the end of the day. A shameless indulgence! I wait for it. I crave it. I sneak it! It makes me happy!

Secret Love

There is only one pleasure that will get me
through a bad hair day,
a traffic nightmare,
puffy eyes,
low self-esteem,
vulnerability,
an upcoming birthday.
It never disappoints.
Always pleases,
lasts a long time.
Thank you,
Mrs. See's for
making
chocolate See's suckers!

11

Celebrating the Fabric of Life

*"Getting older is a lot of fun, right up there with
chewing glass and putting your hand in a blender."*

ALBERT BROOKS

I THINK WE SHOULD commemorate everything—
birthdays, anniversaries, and holidays of all
kinds. We should also honor a good haircut, a surprise call from a friend, an unexpected check, and
waking up. We never know what's waiting for us.
Let's celebrate today.

The fabric of life is made of deep friendships, loving family, girlfriends who have gone all through life
with you, and trying whatever it is you've longed to
do. If you try everything that interests you, there is
no way to fail. Simply trying is winning. And that de-
serves celebration, too.

Family? I'm so proud to be a member of my family.
We might bicker over where we should meet for lunch,
but if anything big happens—good or bad—to any of
us, we are right there. Family means everything to me.

And friends? Show everyone you love that you
mean it. Be there for them as they are there for you.

Let the circle get smaller but stronger.

Of course, milestone birthdays deserve celebration. When I turned eighty, my kids and husband wanted me to have an intimate meaningful dinner with Montecito friends. I hemmed and I hawed, and I finally acquiesced. Why was I hesitating? Gorgeous flowers, beautiful music, a tear-jerking video of my life? Wonderful food and so many touching tributes from my family? What was my problem? Then two old friends had a birthday party for me with only girl-friends I had known since high school. What could have been better?

Celebrating Beverlye's eightieth birthday.

I only wish for myself to have as many powerful moments in my eighties as I had in my seventies. I want to just continue the work I have been lucky enough to do. Because of my illness, many doors opened for me, and I entered places I never dreamed

I'd get to go. I've been so lucky. Because I've been granted these bonus years, I want to continue to pay back as much as I can. I want to stretch myself to another level. And feel worthwhile about my life. The rest will take care itself. Audrey Hepburn said, "We have two hands, one to help ourselves, and one to help others." I endorse that wholeheartedly.

The Girl in the Ermine Stole

I laughed as I walked into my eye doctor's appointment. I was to find out that day if my macular degeneration had become worse. If it hadn't, then I could have cataract surgery. (That would be the good news.) As it turned out, there was no change, so I could either try a new prescription for eyeglasses or have cataract surgery. What a choice!

My choices used to be hike ten miles or play three sets of tennis. What has happened here? Someone has obviously switched bodies and retinas on me. I'm not complaining, just explaining. We're grateful, mind you, that we have these choices, but in our heads we believe we are still in our forties. One minute ago I was the nineeen-year-old girl in the ermine stole, and the next minute I'm talking about cataract surgery.

We have to laugh! Where did time go? Still we have to embrace every new stage we enter. I may have entered my eighties, but I feel like a college freshman, in unexplored territory. I can't wait until my sophomore and junior year to see what lies ahead.

Here are some quotes on aging that I like:

"Youth has no age."
Pablo Picasso

"We are always the same age inside."
Gertrude Stein

"Aging is not lost youth but a new stage of opportunity and strength."
Betty Friedan

"You're never too old to set a new goal or dream a new dream."
C.S. Lewis

"Age puzzles me. I thought it was a quiet time. My 70s were interesting, but my 80s are passionate. I grow more intense as I age."
Thorida Scott Maxwell

"Twenty years from now you will be more disappointed by the things you didn't do than by the ones you did do.
So throw off the bowline
Sail away from the safe harbor
Catch the trade winds in your sails
Explore
Dream
Discover."
Unknown

Remember to play music that you love, put on a pair of high heels once in a while for a morale booster, and dance around the house. Then sail away!

Friends

Helen Keller said, "My friends have made the story of my life." Friends have different meanings for us as we grow up and older (well, maybe not up, just older). When I was very young, I wanted a best friend who was just like me. When I was a young woman, I wanted someone I could trust, someone I could tell all my secrets to. As a young married with small babies, I wanted a friend to share my interests in children, their activities, and their future. Once my children were grown and out of the house, I needed someone to share that empty place in my heart. Our friends may stay the same our whole lives or change from time to time, but our desire for someone who cares, whom we can trust and share our secrets with remains the same.

We want someone who will be with us in "sickness and in health," as in a marriage. We need a soldier in our own personal army who will march by our side until we drop. We have no time for faux friends who only smile at us on a sunny day. We need friends who will gather us up in their arms when the wind is blowing and our hands are numb with cold. The friends who take your hands and breathe on them to warm them. These are the friends to let in your front door and keep in your life forever.

Soup Ingredients

If life were soup, fun would be the chicken, the good stuff you search for at the bottom of the pot. Don't discount fun as frivolous! Fun is one of the major ingredients of life. Fun is the hot fudge on the ice cream and the crispy skin on the potato. Take it in and enjoy it. Chew slowly so you can cherish every bite.

Let's not ever be too tired, too old, too broke, or too sad to have fun. Make room for girlish fun, secret fun, scary fun, outlandish fun. Fun you can't even remember half of, but that has left you smiling just the same. Dancing is fun. Playing poker with my grandchildren is fun. Tequila is fun. More dancing is fun. Sidesplitting belly laughs are fun. Capri is fun. Romance is fun.

Go out and find it. Life can be so serious, we shouldn't ever feel guilty for taking the time to have fun.

The New Forgetting

Forgetting in your forties and fifties is different than forgetting in your later years! Forgetting in your forties means, "Oh, I'm sorry I forgot to call you back last night." Now when I forget, it means that when I go to introduce my husband to a new friend I can't remember either one of their names. It means when I walk into a room I stand there frozen, wondering what I came in for. It means I get into my car to go somewhere and don't remember where I'm going or why. That's forgetting!

I spend half my life looking for my car keys, sunglasses, and purse. Forgetting means I may get a call asking, "Why aren't you here?" while I'm home still sitting in my robe. Worse yet, I may go somewhere only to be asked, "Why are you here?" It takes a village to remember the name of a movie we saw two days ago, the stars who were in it, or where we had dinner afterward. It means you can't come up with the word for what you do with your lips when you pucker up in affection, or whether we are in the month of May or June. It's the scary kind of forgetting. I have a friend who called the police because her car was missing, and when they found it around the corner, she remembered she had left it there!

I recently gave a talk at a retirement home and stayed to chat with everyone. When I came out two hours later, I discovered I had left the motor running in my car.

Oh, well. The only thing that helps is that we are all in this together!

We're in This Together

Remind me about the lunch we have next
week, because I'll never remember
to put it in my iPhone
or look on my computer
where I so diligently put it with an alarm.
Late at night, sitting at my desk,
I wonder: Is it this Thursday
or next Thursday? 12:30 or 1?

Was I supposed to call you first or you call me?
I'll write it on this slip of paper
and put it on my dashboard
and hope I remember to transfer it to
my phone.
I'm late now.
Gotta run.
Have you seen my keys and sunglasses?
They were just here. I just had them. They're
the black glasses I always wear.
But that reminds me to tell you something
before I go.
Wait, I just lost it.
I'll remember it in a minute.
It was about that movie we saw...
what was the name of it again?
Call me when you remember the name of the
movie, and then I'll remember what I wanted
to tell you;
this time I really have to go.
Oh, here are my keys. They were in my purse
and my glasses on top of my head.
Gotta run.
By the way, did you see where I parked
my car?

Passion

I'm not talking about the kind of passion you had at
one point of your life, when you bumped into someone named Antonio at a party in Rome and had three

wonderful days and nights. I'm talking about the kind of passion you have fifty years later for a new kind of love or a cause or a new business or a new art form. The kind of passion that wakes you up in the morning or keeps you up at night and makes you want to continue doing what you love to do.

At this stage in our lives we are not needed as much by our children or even our grandchildren. We love our families, and they love us more than ever, but they have busy lives and so do we. We need to find our passion! They say that if you reach eighty, it's a pretty sure bet you will reach ninety. So there you have it. We need to fill those ten or fifteen years with exploration and a reason to be.

A friend's husband just had his first sculpture exhibition—successfully!—at ninety. It doesn't matter how old you are; it's time to reinvent.

I have been lucky, in that writing and photography have returned to my life after many years. I have fallen in love with taking photos of rocks, stones, driftwood, sunsets, and anything on the beach. They show me how aging can be beautiful. Who knows what I will want to take photos of after that? I love writing, too. My brain is also constantly thinking of words. I want to hear and tell everyone's story. I want to know how everyone feels about aging. And I want to tell the world how I feel about what hurts us and what helps us.

There is something new waiting for all of us. It may be a needle in a haystack, but it is worth looking for. Put on your high heels (metaphorically, of course) and find it. Look for your passion! Reinvention is the name of the game at this stage of our lives.

There is only excitement and fulfillment to gain.

Nelson Mandela said, "It always seems impossible until it's done." He was right.

12

Traveling

TRAVELING IS DIFFERENT as we grow older. Terminals seem longer, arrival and departure dates are harder to keep track of. Tickets, passports, and boarding passes keep disappearing. It's just not the same. Shall we start with the dress code? In 1954, when I went on my honeymoon to Hawaii on a Pan American Clipper, I wore my pink wool high-waisted "going-away suit" from Matthews in Beverly Hills. I believe I even wore white gloves. My sister and I spent endless hours discussing what I should wear on the plane.

The flight from Los Angeles to Oahu was eleven hours, but what did I care? The plane had a downstairs dining room with tablecloths, and the stewardesses (as they were called then) served us our long and delicious meal. How exciting and glamorous it was! All the foreign airlines were elegant, too. The first time I stepped onto an Air France plane I was enchanted. The "stewards" brought the serving cart down the aisle with rare wines and roast beef ready to carve. It was hard not to fall in love with travel.

Today the dress code is more casual, to say the

least; shorts, tank tops, and flip-flops are the uniform. Well-dressed people are in jeans and a T-shirt—and that includes me and my husband. I admit it's more comfortable but, oh, I miss that wonderful era— the anticipation, the glamour, and the service. On a no-frills airline today, feather pillows cost five dollars, and Fritos will set you back three. That's a long way from downstairs dining rooms.

On a flight to Milan (the airline shall remain nameless) the meals were mystery food, and it was obvious that Gwyneth Paltrow didn't design the menu. The "flat beds" that were supposed to be so perfect for sleeping were like caskets; you slid under the seat in front of you. Not appealing.

I still want to go and see places, but I must admit, not as much as before. My dog, my rocks, and my dolphins are all looking pretty good to me. And, by the way, I'd rather cook a chicken at home, and the pillows are free. But when Capri calls, it's hard not to answer.

Men Don't Do That

I know this is a First World problem, but before a European trip, this is how I pack: I begin by bringing out a rack and everything I think I might want to take. I try the clothes on and discuss my choices with girlfriends. Then I try to start eliminating. Do you think I should take the black leather jacket for Paris? It might get cold. Wear it with white pants or black pants and a scarf? How many scarves? What about shoes? They're always a problem. Walking on cobblestones in high heels? I don't think so. But I still need shoes with some kind of heel to make me feel feminine at night. These questions go around and around in my brain.

My husband just sits and watches this in amazement. He listens; he watches; he naps; he shakes his head. I buy and return shoes, pants, and tops until the last item has been altered or returned. At the last minute I throw in a couple of extra sweaters that I know I cannot live without. What should I wear on the plane? Comfort before all else! But still I want to look fairly nice. If we're going to two different kinds of places—Capri, a resort, and Paris, a metropolis—I need different clothes for each. Then there are cosmetics, medicines, shampoos, conditioner, and so on. Those I pack in plastic bags. My room stays a mess for two weeks as I take clothes from the rack and put others in their places. Before we moved to our condo full time, my husband had never seen this process before. He was baffled.

Two days before we leave, my husband presses a couple of shirts and a couple of pairs of jeans, brings out a sport jacket and two pairs of shoes, throws them into a suitcase, and he's ready to go. A neighbor stopped by and, after looking at my rack of clothes, said casually, "Oh yeah, men don't do that!"

Bella Capri

My husband bought me the most wonderful gift for a recent European trip. The gift of comfort! It came in the form of chartreuse Saucony walking shoes! I know I write about aging in high heels, and I did wear some heels at night, but during the day, I flew around in my chartreuse bombers. If I went to the beach or to the pool, I wore sandals, but those walking shoes saved my life! No blisters! No sore spots!

Let's face it, traveling is hard. It's plain hell, actually. The problem is that after you arrive and you love it, you forget how hard it was to get there: Los Angeles to London Heathrow. Drive to Gatwick. Sleep at the airport overnight. Get up at 4:30 a.m. to catch a plane to Naples, and then a hydrofoil to Capri. Whew!!!!

We arrived on a glorious day, tired but hopeful. My mouth was watering for one of those sumptuous breakfasts on the terrace, baskets filled with crunchy bread! My heart skipped a beat at my first sight of Capri. We hadn't been back for six years, and it truly is the most heart-stoppingly beautiful place in the world.

At the dock, Sergio from the Hotel Scalinatella met us with a smile to take our luggage up to the hotel. Meanwhile we jumped on the funicular because we love the view of the island from there. Then came that familiar walk to the hotel, through the piazza, and past the shops, as we wondered if the same staff would still be at the hotel. Franco, Gennaro, Maurizio, the owner Nik. Would they remember us?

We arrived just in time for a gorgeous lunch around the pool. As we walked in, Gennaro looked up and said, "I don't believe it. Madame, Mr. Fead, welcome back!"

The Scalinatella is not just any hotel; it feels like a private club. The staff has been here for thirty or forty years, and they know everyone and their likes and dislikes. The guests have been coming for forty years, too, and everyone knows everyone (in a good way). Lunches are long and delicious with eight or ten people laughing as the wine is poured.

In Capri.

Other guests introduced us to wonderful people from London, Brazil, Geneva, and Paris. Joseph (a guest whom I consider the unofficial mayor of the Scalinatella) would ask, "Shall we go to the beach tomorrow?" Yes, of course. Or he would ask, "Shall we go to Faraglioni's for dinner tonight?" Of course.

Everywhere you go, you're thrilled by the beauty. The bougainvillea drips over aged stones. Huge rocks stand tall and strong in the sparkling sea, that beautiful, blue-green sea.

Then there are the shops. Don't get me started! Every cashmere sweater, pair of shoes, piece of jewelry, and exquisite dress you ever wanted is waiting for you to take them home. You have to be strong!

So is it worth it to travel all that way, with all those inconveniences? For us, yes!

How lucky we were to go one more time.

Why, Oh Why, Do I Love Paris?
Because the Foie Gras There

We took an early morning flight from Naples to Paris, saying goodbye to one beloved spot and saying hello to another. We threw our bags down in our lovely suite at our favorite little Left Bank hotel, Duc de Saint-Simon, and immediately walked to the Café de Flore on Boulevard Saint Germain and ordered foie gras, crunchy bread, and rosé wine. Because we were still hungry, we asked for goat cheese and more crunchy bread. That set the tone for the trip. We ate as much bread, foie gras, and goat cheese as was humanly possible in five days. The rest of the trip consisted of trying new bistros, walking, shopping, and eating more crunchy bread.

Paris never disappoints. I felt like I was in a Woody Allen film. Wherever I walked, I could hear his narration and the wonderful music he uses. At one point we saw a young man playing the piano in front of the Musée d'Orsay? How Woody Allen was that?

I had been gluten free, alcohol free, and dairy free for two years, and it was as though I had been let out of prison. I ate and drank everything! We were in heaven. By far my favorite eating spot was L'Atelier de Joel Robuchon. Paul Bert and L'AOC were tied for second, with their marvelous cheese platters, superb bread, and bistro fare, including a wonderful blood sausage. We tried to go only to new places, but we couldn't resist Les Deux Magots or Café de Flore; we were at one of them for breakfast every day.

In Paris.

One particular night was music night in Paris, and there were bands all over the city. At Paul Bert, we were lucky enough to have gypsies sing and play as only they can do. We stopped to see beautiful art, but our timing was off and the lines were too long, so we never got into a museum.

All the streets on the Left Bank are filled with wonderful stores, each chock full of unusual goodies. But if you are a shopper, just go right to Bon Marché. We spent a couple of hours there, and it wasn't half enough. Not enough hours, not enough time to do everything.

But we hadn't come with an agenda. We just did what we wanted to do. The combination of the beautiful architecture, the Seine, the parks, the art, and the food makes this place magical. Paris does more than fill just your stomach. It also fills your soul. At this stage in our lives, that's what it takes.

13

Loss

"Bad things do happen; how I respond to them defines my character and the quality of my life. I can choose to sit in perpetual sadness, immobilized by the gravity of my loss, or I can choose to rise from the pain and treasure the most precious gift I have—life itself."

WALTER ANDERSON

I'M NOT TALKING ABOUT the impossible-to-comprehend loss of a mate or child. Somehow the ones left behind are expected to go on and recover from it, but I know not how.

What I'd like to discuss is the bad-enough, life-changing loss of a parent, sibling, or dear friend. This kind of loss leaves a hole that can be covered over, but underneath something remains empty forever. Lately I find that I even mourn people I don't know. I read their names in the obituaries and see their faces. It says they left a wife or husband, two or three children, and four or five grandchildren. I can picture their life. I can see how hard they worked, and how they tried to make their life count for something. How they tried to make a difference in this world. And I know how difficult it is for their family.

I've lost so many dear ones in my life: my parents, my two sisters, close relatives, and lifelong friends. Their presence is always with me, and I feel them guiding me. But the pain of the loss has remained. I never stop missing them or wishing I could see their faces or hear their voices.

As we enter this third age, we are unfortunately on a first-name basis with loss. Our friends are beginning to leave us. Someone said, "They are calling up our class." Maybe that's true. I'd like to think they are leaving this existence to go to the next level. One we don't know about, but that we can imagine any way we like. I imagine it to be beautiful with people we love waiting for us. That's what I choose to believe. And that's what gets me through!

More to Learn

I had two new diagnoses not long ago. One was myelodysplasia (MDS), which is a low white blood count. While this sounds like it's serious—and someday could be—it just has to be watched and needs nothing but blood tests for now. Whew! It's the other diagnosis that has my attention: psoriasis! Remember the "heartbreak of psoriasis"? Well, it *is* a heartbreak! I understand that old commercial now.

The spots began mostly on my legs, and then they crept up to my arms and shoulders. They kept changing shapes and colors, and they were horrible to look at, red and big! For someone who was taught that looks were everything, this was tough. And no one could figure out what they were.

I took prednisone, the spots grew worse. We went on a trip, the spots got worse. We tried antibiotics, creams, ointments, and sprays. They all had their own side effects, yet nothing seemed to do the trick. I worried all the time, wondering where they were going next—face, eyes, everywhere.

This is where my husband shines. He is nurturing and supportive. Every night he held my hand and said, "We're going to get to the bottom of this and take care of it, Bev." Still, I felt vulnerable. The spots made me feel I was sick every time I looked down. I thought, this is not a blip in the road. This is a rut!

Finally, though, the doctors got a definitive diagnosis, and out of several possible treatments, I chose the "light box." Three times a week, for fifteen weeks, I would stand in a booth (like tanning) and get narrow-band ultraviolet rays for about 1½ minutes.

Just as I did with cancer, I've now entered a whole new world with heroic people in it. When I sat waiting for the "box," I found myself in the middle of a spontaneous support group. We would tell each other our remedies and successes. It really helped! This person had lived with it for fifteen years. That one's father had it all his life. This one has had it for five years, and on and on. Everyone had some kind of remedy for me: "Don't eat nightshades." "Take oatmeal baths," and so on. They also had some horrible stories that kept me up at night. But these people taught me they were all living a regular life with smiles on their faces; psoriasis was just a part of it. Not all of it! Okay. I get it. It can be done. After two years my spots have improved enormously, and it seems, with what I have learned, I can control them.

We're never too old to learn and change courses, right? It's not what you're given but how you handle what you're given that matters. I'm not caving in to spots! Or a low white-blood-cell count for that matter, and looks aren't everything (but we knew that). And by the way, this is just another blip in the road after all.

The Dalai Lama said, "We can let the circumstances of our lives harden us so that we become increasingly resentful and afraid, or we can let them soften us, and make us kinder. We always have the choice."

Psoriasis will get no more tears from me!

God's Hands

We live in a scary world. There is no question about it. Maybe every generation has thought that. As I grow older, I think more and more about needing some help—a higher power or whatever we want to call it. I know it has been said before, but I am just now coming around to believe that there are times we have to let go, throw up our hands, and leave it to the gods.

The doctor told me my life was in God's hands.
When we fly, we are in God's hands.
When we step across the street, we are in God's hands.
I think he/she's not a person but some type of all-encompassing
being that takes care of our problems across the universe.
Oh, I admit he's slow on the uptake on some,
but still I feel something, somehow, is there to help us.
I picture a pair of cupped hands holding me
right in the middle of massive fingers.
It is a comforting feeling.
And until proved wrong,
that is what I believe.
I feel it is easier
if we believe in something to help us
through this very terrifying, death-defying, lovely
life in which we live.

14
Never Too Late

LATELY, I HAVE been talking to small groups around town. I find it very rewarding, and I like the feeling of sitting down and having a conversation afterward. One particular group, the "Monday Group," has been meeting every Monday for fifty years, I figured the women had to be in their seventies.

My friend Kerin, who is a member and definitely the baby of the group, asked if I would speak to them. I had no idea what to expect. I went there a little early and was able to talk one-on-one with some of the ladies. I told the first woman, proudly, how old I was (expecting a little pat on the back), and she said, "That's nice, dear; I'm ninety-four!" What? I thought? She had a vital, intelligent look in her eyes, and so did all the others.

They were eighty-five, eighty-seven, ninety-one, ninety-four. And all of them were interested and interesting. After my talk, they asked thought-provoking questions that I enjoyed answering. What a preview into the late eighties and nineties they gave me. They made it look easy and definitely not scary. It was all that curiosity that helped them stay so young.

Some of them had canes, and most had replacements of body parts. A few had had serious illnesses. Some had lost spouses and even children, but they were grateful to be there and to be with one another. They all said that in one way or another. The feeling that I took away from that day was that it's never too late to learn and how friends play a major role in our lives.

What a meaningful morning. I came there to inspire them with my story, but I walked away being inspired by theirs!

Poet Samuel Ullman wrote, "Nobody grows old merely by living a number of years. We grow old by deserting our ideals. Years may wrinkle the skin, but to give up enthusiasm wrinkles the soul."

What Are We Supposed to Do?

One thing that puzzles me is what we are supposed to do at this stage of our lives. I spend a great deal of my time thinking about that.

Are we supposed to see all the things we always wanted to see? Are we supposed to work as hard and as fast as possible as we sprint to the finish line? Should we do as much as we can for others to make a better life for them? Or just relax, spend time with family and friends and make a better life for ourselves? Do we need to keep reinventing? Or do we try to complete our circle by doing just a little bit of all of the above?

Part of my frustration is that I've always done a

little bit of this and a little bit of that, and have not kept to a straight line. When I read about a boy who knew at eight that he wanted to be an actor or a girl who knew at twelve that she wanted to be a doctor, I wonder: What could an eight- or twelve-year old possibly know about what they want to be in their thirties? How lucky for them!

I guess I'm saying I'm not that focused, and I only have so many years to decide what I want to be when I grow up (which may never happen). How do we make sure we spend our time on this earth wisely? Our time is precious. We all want to leave this planet a better place for generations to come, but how much time should we spend on that? And what would make the most difference?

I sit and wonder. Maybe *that's* what we're supposed to do.

Excess

Excess isn't always a bad thing. At Thanksgiving there was an excess of eating, love, good feelings, and gratitude. And it was all good!

It started off Wednesday night with baking and excessive eating of ribs and chicken at the home of my son and daughter-in law. The Thanksgiving meal was plentiful. There were ten of us, and together we cooked a sumptuous turkey, with stuffing and all the trimmings at my daughter's house. Gratitude was never far from our minds.

The family (from bottom row)—
Terry, Beverlye, Bob, Alex, Gideon, Tessa, Jim, and Leslie.

Late in the evening I discovered the peanut brittle. More excess. Friends of the family came over with their kids, and there was an excess of laughing, too.

The next night we celebrated Bob's eightieth birthday, and that was the first time we could all remember his children, my children, and our grandchildren together. There wasn't a dry eye as we celebrated Bob's life in speeches and photos filled with love and admiration.

My husband said it was the best night of his life. How could that be anything but good? We all had the most wonderful time together!

So my theory is to let the good times roll, ignore the tight pants, and enjoy excesses whenever possible. He certainly deserved it, and so did we!

I wasn't sorry about any of the excesses (except maybe the pound of peanut brittle).

15

Lists

Ten Things We Are Willing to Give Up

1. Traveling to remote places that take three days to reach and two months to recover from.
2. Pretenses. We don't need BS anymore.
3. Friendships that tire us out with too much pressure and not enough laughs and understanding.
4. Sleeveless, backless, strapless dresses. Let's face it, we just want to show our face, and if veils were popular we'd wear them too.
5. Going braless. Don't make me laugh.
6. Bikinis…unless you are in your closet with the lights off.
7. Sexy nightwear. I prefer T-shirts, the older and smoother the better.
8. Five-star dinners. No more tasting menus that last for four hours.
9. Talking and drinking the night away. I'm no longer willing to wake up feeling lousy the next morning.
10. Going across town—any town—at ten o'clock at night to see something or someone.

However, all these rules are meant to be broken. At this time of our life, if we want to go to a remote place, then we should just do it. If we want to wear a strapless dress, again, do it. We don't need to ask permission, we don't need to worry about it, we no longer need approval. We just get to do it.

That to me is aging in high heels.

Ten Things We Are Not Willing to Give Up

1. Family. As time goes on, family gets more meaningful every day.
2. Friends we cherish. Girlfriends—the ones who give and take, listen and talk, care and accept care—become more and more important in our lives.
3. Music of all kinds. It's crucial for our mood and our inspiration.
4. Great easy dinners at home with the fire blazing, husband, TV, dog, and, occasionally, friends.
5. Holiday dinners with family and friends, cooking, kids, music, and dogs. Everything we love.
6. Some form of expression, as in painting, writing, photography, cooking, singing—whatever says, this is what I see; this is who I am.
7. Different ways of giving back—whatever it takes to fulfill you and helps others.
8. Computers and cell phones. I admit it, I'm hooked!

9. Beach walks or hiking in the mountains. Good for the head and the soul.

10. Chocolate. Self-explanatory. Preferably dark chocolate bark with nuts. Or See's chocolate suckers. Yum!

What's better than a beach walk with a loved one, dinner at home, and chocolate bark for dessert? Nothing I can think of!

16
Remembering Us

Don't you think I remember what it's like to be you?
No time, everything is rushed.
I meant to call, but didn't.
Yes, I looked at the clock, just had no time.
Now I have all the time in the world.
I'm not mad, just miss when I could smell your hair
and you fit in my arms,
depended on me,
waited for me,
laughed with me
Don't you think I remember?

17
Lonely Is a Good Thing

LONELY: sad because one has no friends or company. Synonyms: isolated, alone, lonesome, friendless, with no one to turn to, forsaken, abandoned, rejected, unloved, unwanted, outcast, depressed, desolate, forlorn, cheerless, down, blue.

Does loneliness hit only when you are by yourself? I don't think so! Sometimes being by myself is the loveliest thing that can happen. Reading, taking photos on the beach, or writing—all activities I do alone—make me feel happy.

To be lonely is more than that. The sense of feeling alone may hit while you're surrounded by the people you love. Inexplicably you still feel lonely and not included. It is the feeling in the pit of your stomach that grabs you in the middle of a sleepless night or when you glimpse a young family walking by with the children looking up at the parents so adoringly. It can hit when you see lovers at a restaurant or an older couple sitting in the park.

Loneliness is always an unexpected guest. Somehow I feel the sense of loneliness more as I grow older. No matter how fast I run, I can't seem to outrun it. I think it has something to do with the stage of life we are in. No matter how long this last stage will be, we know we will have to do the last leg alone. However, I believe that thought is empowering.

You get to choose if your path is rough or smooth. It's up to us how being alone makes us feel.

18
Firsts

I BUMPED INTO a friend of mine at the pharmacy the other day, and she told me that after her husband passed away, she was not happy in her big house. She decided to scale down and get a much smaller place in a retirement community. Her eyes lit up with excitement as she talked. It was a first for her. She would have her own house just the way she liked it. She looked forward to it.

Another friend told me that she was going to take Pilates for the first time, and she, too, was very excited. It's gratifying to reach out and try something different, go to new places, sing a different song. It's something we must all strive for as we grow older, because we get so comfortable with the things we know.

A woman I respect very much asked me if I would be interviewed on video for a new project she was working on. She continues to reinvent herself and is loaded with firsts. So of course I agreed and found it to be a terrific experience.

I had so many firsts in my seventies, I want to keep finding new ones in my eighties, and, God willing, into my nineties. The good news is the more I look, the more I find.

If a first comes to you, I hope you grab it with both hands, treasure it, and run with it as fast as you can.

Clutter

My desk is a mess! It's full of invitations, a computer, a calendar, artifacts, stamps, envelopes, a camera, post-its, and general clutter. Folders lie on a table next to my desk, and every time I get up from the desk, I bump into the folders, and they fall. I'd like to make all that disappear.

I build in cabinets. I have shelves and organizers. I hire people, and they put things in places never to be seen again! I always think the next person who comes is going to solve the problem, but secretly I know the problem is me. Can an old dog learn new tricks?

I did have some new cabinets made, and it helped a great deal. I was thrilled at thought of sitting at my desk, working on the computer in an area that was totally organized. No post-its all over my desk. A serene space. (I still have several partially used notebooks, however.)

Ommmmmmmmm.

19
The Eternal Optimist

BESIDES GETTING married at nineteen and having babies right away, there was another reason I didn't go back to UCLA and get my degree. Fear of written tests! Oh, how I would sweat it out! You could show me anything and explain it, and I would understand. But to read something, understand it, and then be tested? Panic! I even had a girlfriend take a test for me once at school. What were we thinking?

As adults, we have very few written tests to worry about. One, however, is mandatory. And it is scary. The driver's license written test. I hated the very thought. It had never bothered me before, but the last time I faced it I was nervous. I thought if they realized I was eighty, and I flunked it a few times (you're only allowed three tries), they would not give me a license again. Then what?

I studied online and went in, head held high, to take the test. You could only miss three answers and still pass. I missed four. I flunked! The woman grading the tests had all the warmth of a jail warden in Mississippi. I think I made her day. But I was horrified. I made a return appointment and went home to study.

Day and night, I studied. The tension mounted. There is no doubt there are tricky questions on the test, but I'm not dumb, I kept telling myself. I took the practice tests online and did fine, but that didn't give me confidence. I continued to study.

The appointed day came, and I went to the DMV. Ahead of me was a nice little old lady (permed white hair and stretch pants). Grading the tests was a sweet new guy, but behind him was The Warden.

The little old lady said to me, "I'm nervous; they are very tricky, you know." I could feel my heart beat a little faster. I (the eternal optimist) replied, "Let's hope we both pass!"

We got our tests and went to the booths to take them. My test didn't seem so hard this time. Near the end, however, were two questions that I agonized over. I finally put in answers and got into the line with The Warden, the new sweet guy, and my older lady friend. She was two people ahead of me, which meant that she had finished fast. I heard The Warden tell her, "You only missed one, dear, congratulations!"

The pressure was on. I studied my test again, while the next person in line was graded. Then I went back in the booth and changed one of the answers I had agonized over. Finally, it was my turn.

The Warden and the sweet new guy looked at my test and went down the answers. It seemed to take a long time. Finally I asked, "Did I pass?"

"Yes, you only missed two," said the new guy. (One of those was an answer I had changed at the last minute; my first answer was right after all.) I was thrilled and relieved, "You are doing such a good job," I said to the new guy. *What the hell,* I thought… and to The Warden, I added, "and you are doing a wonderful job of instructing him." They both smiled.

You see? I said to myself. I'm not old!

The next morning I woke up and threw my dirty socks in the wastepaper basket and my Kleenex in the dirty-clothes hamper. I laughed when I realized what I had done.

That could happen to anyone, thought the eternal optimist.

20
Night Hopes

WHEN I LIE IN BED in the still of the night and think about the past (oh, yes, I know how dangerous that is), I try to forgive myself for only knowing what I knew at that time. We learn as we get older, but even so we continue to make stupid mistakes. There are sentences we wish we could take back and actions we pray weren't as bad as we remember them. How many of us have clicked "send" and then hoped our computer would die before our email actually went through?

I remember saying to my mother, who was hard of hearing, "No, I'm not going to repeat that, because it loses something if you have to repeat it." Today I cringe at my carelessness with her feelings. Now I'm the one asking, "What?" and expecting everyone to patiently repeat themselves. We all end up depending on the kindness of strangers in one way or another.

Robert Frost was asked, at the end of his life, if he had hope for the future. He answered, "Yes, and even for the past…that it will turn out to have been all right for what it was. Something I can accept. Mistakes made by the self I had to be or was not able to be."

How comforting that is to me!

Who Would Know?

I talk to Sleep at night,
my elusive friend.
I lie in wait to talk to him.
I'm so tired,
my eyes so heavy,
my legs are crampy.
Who would it hurt
if you gave me just a little?
Who would know?
I'll wait for you forever.
Like a foolish lover,
I'll keep running after you
until I find you.
Come on, Sleep…
just one deep kiss.

21
Is There an Afterlife?

*"When I stand before God at the end of my life,
I would hope that I would not have a single bit
of talent left and could say, 'I used everything you
gave me.'"*

ERMA BOMBECK

IN MY HEART I have always believed there was an afterlife, and now I'm convinced. My daughter-in-law, as part of an extravagant birthday present, had a psychic come to her house to give me and a few members of the family a group reading. What an amazing gift! I know it sounds very woo-woo, but this man said things and mentioned names that the ordinary person wouldn't have known. I believe there are people with powers to see and hear and be in touch with people from the other side, and I believe there is another life we go to from here. I think of it as being very beautiful and peaceful, a place where we are surrounded by people and things we love. I picture that place having trailing bougainvillea and white roses, Latin music playing, and clear turquoise water nearby.

Is that Pollyannaish? Maybe. But until someone comes up with proof that once we die, that is all there is, I'm going to go on believing that we transition to another world.

The psychic also told me that I wouldn't be seeing that beautiful place for a long, long time! So I'm back to thinking about what I really want to do with my life in my eighties and my nineties. There's so much I want to do.

I know I want to give back, speak, and inspire. I know I want to continue writing and taking photos. I know I want to let people know that aging and illnesses are different today from the way they used to be. We have help from all over the world and so much information. We live in an amazing era.

Now that I think about it, the place I live has bougainvillea, beautiful blue water nearby, and people I love. So I'm not in a hurry to go anywhere just yet. I'm still busy and excited here on earth.

22
That Old Hand

She placed my hand
On the x-ray plate.
"Do this," she said. And situated
her hand next to mine.
We looked at our hands together.
We saw the skin and fingers of
an older woman
next to a smooth young hand,
like that of a department store mannequin.
I felt sad for my old hand.
"I'm sorry," I said to it inside my head.
"There's nothing I can do about it."
"Don't worry," my hand answered back.
"It's not all bad. Don't forget
that old hand just wrote this poem."

23
Age Related

SO HERE WE ARE, aging in high heels, dancing as fast as we can. I don't know which is falling faster, my face or my derriere. There's nothing we can do about it. I hike. I walk. I do everything one is supposed to do, but gravity is working faster than I am. We just have to look at the whole aging process as a joke. We need to be grateful we are here and able to dance at all.

Where Are They?

Has anyone seen my looks?
They seem to have disappeared.
They could belong to any woman of
a certain age.
Is that fair?
The hair surrounding this new face
has become flat and wooly,
my eyes puffed and beady.
Do I have to take this lying down?
Is this how I'm meant to go through
the rest of my life?

Where did my other face go?
I'm just curious.
Who has taken it?

There are all kinds of ways to look at our bodies as we enter our fifties, sixties, and seventies, and yes, even beyond that. We can torture ourselves comparing our looks now to what we used to look like or to the young women in the pages of *Vogue* and *Harper's Bazaar*. Or we can be realistic and think of all the wisdom that comes with the wrinkles. It's not a bad trade-off.

Foot Faults

I was at a luncheon the other day with some friends, and we were all dressed with our high heels on. Three of us started complaining about our feet, and we took off our shoes to play "show and tell." One of us had toes that went in two different directions, another had a foot shaped like a crescent moon, and the third had corns on top of every toe. What could we do but laugh? And we did. (Otherwise we'd cry.) It gave us comfort to know we were all in this together. But don't feel sorry for us or turn off the music yet because we're not through dancing, and we're definitely still having a great time!

I never would have guessed that it was going to be my feet that would betray me. You can replace hips, knees, even a heart or a liver, but feet? I don't think so. I'm afraid this all falls under the heading of the two dreaded words one hears after a certain birthday.

"Age related," says the doctor as he studies the chart. There is no cure for anything that is age related. It can apply to a myriad of ailments. I get it. Accept, adjust, and move on once again.

Oh, my poor crooked-toed feet. Now I have a new searing pain in my instep that is trying to keep me from high heels, dancing, and hiking. But no deal, feet, those are things that are part of me. My shoes may be getting uglier, but that's my only concession. Feet, don't fail me now. I need you to last another ten years. I'll do shots, procedures, whatever it takes.

We cannot let age-related ailments get to us. When a doctor looks at us and says, "Age related," we say, "Not me" and walk away. He doesn't know who we are.

> I never thought
> I would age
> in a cloud of cliché.
> But
> I must confess,
> in my lifetime,
> I've been
> highlighted,
> botoxed,
> Pilatesed,
> and sliced.
> I've been made up,
> brought down,

padded, and slimmed.
I've married
and
divorced.
Parented,
grandparented,
complained,
and supported.
I've hiked
and biked,
tennised and golfed.
At this time of my life
I'm ready to say,
no matter what I do, or
how hard I try,
only my spirit remains young.
My body is just a vessel.

Clockwise from top left: Beverlye at about age three; Mom and Dad dancing at Beverlye's wedding; dancing with Dad on Beverlye's thirteenth birthday; before Beverlye's first art exhibit; Bob Fead with his daughter, Laurel, and son, Michael; with daughter, Terry, and son, Jim, at her fiftieth birthday party; the Fisher sisters—Eileen, Thelma, and Beverlye—in the early 1940s.

Clockwise from top left: At a book signing for Nana, What's Cancer?; *with Bob; Bob's grandson and daughter-in-law, Jackson and Tera Fead; taking photos on the beach in Montecito; speaking in Washington, D.C.; Terry with her daughter, Tessa; Bob's grandson Max Clark; Jim with his wife, Leslie, and sons, Gideon and Alex.*

24
Do What You Want To

A GIRLFRIEND SENT ME a video called *Slomo*, and it was not only interesting to watch, but it also provoked a great deal of discussion among my husband, myself, and our friends. "Slomo" was a successful doctor for many years, until he noticed he was having some issues with his vision. He also had begun asking himself how much he was getting out of life spiritually. Coincidentally he ran into an older man, ninety-three years of age, and he asked him, "What should I be doing to turn myself into a happy man of ninety-three?" The man replied, "Do what you want to!"

"Slomo" felt that was the most profound thing he had ever heard. He sold his cars (a Ferrari and a BMW), his mansion, and everything else, and rented a studio apartment at the beach, and started skating. Yes, skating. Skating became his entire life. He had enough money to live simply, and from then on all he did from morning to night was skate.

At first he thought he had gone crazy, but then he realized he had just thrown away all aggravations. All he needed to make himself happy was to skate.

When I first showed the video to my husband, he asked me, "Do you want me to be Slomo?" (The title comes from skating in slow motion.)

"No," I said, "but isn't he lucky he found his bliss? Isn't that what we are all looking for?"

"Slomo" actually has a scientific explanation for his feeling of happiness, something about how the gravitational force that takes you downhill gives you a feeling of confidence and elation, similar to that of skiing and surfing. I envy this man. He doesn't get sore shoulders at the end of the day or get irritated by little things or need to meditate. He is "doing what he wants to."

Is he crazy or lucky or smart? I think he is lucky to have enough money to live the rest of his life the way he wants, and he is smart to have found something that makes him totally happy and not care what others think. People may find him crazy or, at least, unrealistic. My husband said, "Realistically, we could never live our lives like that." I realize that. In reality, ninety-nine people out of a hundred could not do anything like that. But, oh! if we only could, how easy life would be. No problems, no bills, no meetings, no traffic—just bliss.

"Do what you want to," the old man had said. Can't we do our own version of that? Let's give away more and more the older we get! What do we really need anyway? We don't have to skate, but I sure want "Slomo's" big smile on my face. He has inspired me to keep searching for my own form of bliss.

High five, "Slomo," high five!

The Elder Tree

I don't remember what it's like to be young anymore.
I don't understand what they think, or speak,
but they don't know what it is like to be older either.
Sometimes I get upset because hands don't open jars,
eyes can't read signs,
ears don't hear the words.
It's the new normal,
and I'm grateful for it.
It's a small price to pay for finding out what real
friendship means.
How would I explain the feelings of someone eighty
years on this planet to them?
Do they even need to know?
If this is old age,
bring it on.
Watch us!
We can do this too.

25
Tell Them What You Want

W HEN I WAS in my middle twenties, my mother
was diagnosed with colon cancer. We didn't say
the word "cancer" out loud then. We whispered it. It
was like you had a contagious disease. No one wanted
to drink out of your cup. You had a dirty secret. I did
hear certain words, like "platelets" and "white blood
cells," but I never asked any questions. I was never
told anything. My mother had an operation; she had
treatment. Only later did I realize it must have been
chemotherapy. But she kept getting weaker.

My children were five and seven years old then,
and I carpooled with other mothers and their children. Yet I never told any of my friends about my
mother's illness. It seemed I was always at the hospital
and crying a lot. I wasn't sleeping well. I'd be anxious
about my mother, imagining that her mortality and
mine were mixed up together, and I would feel faint.
I went from doctor to doctor to find out what was
wrong with me. Of course, I was fine. I was just scared
and unable to face my mother's imminent death.

One day my mother had a crisis in the hospital,
and it took up all my brain space. I totally forgot it

was my carpool day and left all the children at school. When they finally tracked me down, they told me the kids had had to wait an hour and a half before they could arrange for another mother to come and pick them up. They were crying and scared, and I had left them out in the cold. I felt horrible.

I had never said, "I need some help" to anyone. I had tried to act as though life were running as usual. But it wasn't. I wasn't. I needed help. And my friends did help me with my children once I told them. They were happy to do so. My mother never recovered, and sadly she died the next year. But I learned something that day. It's okay to tell people what you need. If you don't tell anyone what you want, how will they know?

Hindsight

I thought I was old when I wrote this poem, and now, more than ten years later, I feel I've become younger, wiser, and more spirited. I've dipped my toe in new waters many times in the last few years and found it exhilarating. I thrive on that. We have to live life with abandon at this stage of our lives. What do we have to lose? When I leave this earth, I want to be remembered as someone who was fearless and pursued my dreams. I want all the wishes on my list crossed off.

I hope I can look back at this when I'm about to turn ninety and think *"What a kid I was!"*

Hindsight
I remember when I thought thirty was old.
Then I thought fifty was a fresh start, and now
I think, here I am at seventy, a baby tadpole.
I dip my toe in fresh waters,
to take new chances, new risks.
I see life through wise eyes
with a touch of abandon.
I like this feeling of irreverence.
It thrills me,
this not caring
if I fail.
The only failing is
not dipping the toe in.
The rest is an assured
gold medal.

26
Calendar Reflections

I sit and wonder where the days have gone.
I try to catch the light as it begins to fade
into that beautiful silky red sky,
then wait for the blue black of the night.
I sneak up on the mirror
to grab a fast look at
my face turned one day older,
but to no avail.

I stand in front of the calendar and wait
for the pages to turn.
I walk away, and when I come back,
it's a month later.

It's no use, I think, all the systems at work
are quicker than I.
I guess I'll have to let it happen
on its own.
Not my nature.

Summer Sloth

This is what I love in summer: sleeping late, reading, lying in the sun, writing, and taking photos of rocks and tree trunks. Tree trunks convey to me that same weathered beauty and wisdom as do the rocks. They allow us to see that after all they have been through, they stand tall and firm and beautiful.

I also love sunsets at the beach while eating hors d'oeuvres; they are heartbreakingly beautiful. (The sunsets, not the hors d'oeuvres). I love watching all the action in front of us—paddle boarders, dog walkers, surfers, lovers hand in hand.

There are a myriad of joyful things to do and watch on a summer day—for instance, walking up the San Ysidro Trail! A short lovely hike in the late morning before the weather gets too hot.

Different Kinds of Fourths

I thought maybe it was just the end of the year that gave me "the blues," but I've discovered it's any holiday "blues." Holidays remind you of family. Family reminds you of childhood. Childhood reminds you of holidays. And so it goes. It's all a circle.

There were happy Fourths when I was young, sitting on beach blankets with my sisters and my mother and dad in Coronado, watching the fireworks. There were happy Fourths with my kids when they were little in La Costa and at the Sand and Sea Club in Santa Monica. All of us young married couples were with our four- and six-year-old kids watching fireworks. We would hold them in our arms, wrapped up in towels after their swim. There were fireworks at Rancho Park with games, races, and our children running back to jump in our laps to tell us they won. The Fourths in Aspen were huge! I think we celebrated for four days straight, with fireworks, tequila, and parades. What a combination.

Then we had Fourths up here in Montecito, first with friends on a boat right under the spectacular fireworks. Then came our married kids with their little children all dressed up in their Fourth of July T-shirts. We'd start at the early pancake breakfast in the fire station, watch the little parade in Montecito that takes twenty minutes, and end up at Manning Park. There were games, box lunches, and cotton candy. I remember, when we won first prize in a friend's car in the parade, my grandson said, "Well, if we won first prize, where is our trophy?" And at night we would stand on the beach, huddled together for warmth, watching the fireworks.

There are no little kids to watch fireworks with anymore. Everyone is grown up and traveling! But the good news is we now live in a beach community where everyone wants to watch the fireworks. So we're still having food and drinks on the beach with friends. We don't have to drive anywhere, and we get to walk back home as soon as we get cold and can watch the rest of the fireworks on television in bed cuddled up with our dog!

Maybe I'm not blue after all, just a little nostalgic. There's a difference. Blue is looking back with sadness. Nostalgic is looking back with fondness.

There are all kinds of ways to have fun on the Fourth of July. We just have to go with the flow.

Fall in the Emerald City

Everyone has gone home. The summer renters have gone back to Arizona, New York, or Florida. On the beach there are only the surfers, the paddle boarders, the rocks, stones, and me. No dogs catching Frisbees. No large groups of grown-ups with sun hats holding plastic glasses filled with fine wine, walking and talking earnestly to each other. The stretch of sand is so wide at low tide that one can walk forever. Every time I go, I'm dazzled. It is truly as though a curtain has lifted, and there it is: the Emerald City.

Why is it so magical? And why does it make me want to weep? I can't figure it out. There is something about the juxtaposition of the grass, flowers, sand, and rocks. The lone egrets on the rocks, the waves coming and going, and one man running with his dog all make it seem melancholy without it being sad.

When I walk for exercise (with Aretha in my ear), it's different than when I walk with my camera, examining every stone. When I walk with my camera, it is quiet inside my head. I'm looking and listening. I realize that's my meditation. Meditation can come in many forms. Sometimes it's sitting very still, sometimes it's climbing a mountain, and sometimes it's looking at a rock on the beach.

Wes Nisker, a radio commentator and Buddhist meditation instructor, says, "After a few years of meditation practice, we can even learn how to occasionally ignore ourselves. And what relief that can be!"

I can hardly wait!

No Time

The months have run by. Not once have they turned around and asked, "Are you coming?" They just want to finish out the year in record time. They don't care at all what has happened to us this year.

As the year winds down, life is its usual self, but the months keep pestering us. "There is no time to dawdle," they say. "We are speeding to Halloween. Starting to put up the goblin decorations. We have no time to lose."

We only have a minute to catch our breath. And then it's Thanksgiving, all orange and brown with beautiful turkeys and pumpkin pies. That's the time of the year we really have to rush. We have to get ready for the holidays. We have to prepare for the snow, get Santa's suit pressed, put up the tree, and set out the candles. So much to do! Hurry up. There's no time to look back and ask, "Where did the time go?"

Keep up. We are almost at the finish line. The new year will be here any minute. We'll take a deep breath after everyone kisses at the stroke of twelve; then we can all relax.

No time to reflect now, just hurry. And I say, "Wait. I need time to thank the gods and be grateful for this year."

I'm through running.

27
Holiday Thoughts

THE HOLIDAYS ARE SUCH a mixed bag. I have friends celebrating big occasions. I have friends with no family. I have friends with big families. I have friends with a new puppy. I have a friend who had to put her pet down. I have friends who are happily going from one party to another. I have friends laid low with illness. I have friends who are traveling with three generations of family to faraway places.

For me, it's a time to reflect. I'm so grateful that I have a wonderful family and that we can be together for the holidays. We celebrate them all. I remember previous Christmases when my children were little, when they couldn't wait to decorate the tree. When they couldn't stand waiting one more hour for Santa. When they came in our room at five in the morning and announced, "We're ready to open our presents now." All those videos are playing in my head. I can see my grandchildren when they were babies and recall the joys of taking them to visit Santa and surprising them at Hanukkah and Christmas. Now my grandchildren are teenagers. No one is waiting for Santa, except maybe me!

I'd like Santa to bring me a disposition that doesn't

get cranky so easily. I'd also like Santa to remind me to have a happy, grateful outlook every day. I'd love Santa to bring us some peace in the Middle East and, while he is at it, supply food for each hungry child.

The grandchildren—Max, Gideon, Alex, Jackson, and Tessa.

I hope Santa will bring presents to every child who is waiting for him (regardless of whether they are naughty or nice). I wish Santa would help the world out of the mess it is in, fix global warming, and get rid of terrorists. I wish that Santa, in his spare time, would keep my family healthy and happy and make my husband's back pain go away.

Is that too much to ask of Santa? Personally, I think he's up to it.

Joy

One of the great joys about growing older is how happy we all are for our family of friends. As each person turns sixty, sixty-five, seventy-five, eighty, or ninety, we cheer them on with joy. "Look," we say, "we all made it this far."

Every weekend, it seems, someone reaches a milestone and celebrates it. And why shouldn't they? Aches and pains are forgotten as we tell great stories and share familiar laughter. The only thing we can think of is, "We are all still here."

Ten Suggestions for a New Year

1. Throw out your old thoughts, just like you throw out old clothes that no longer fit.
2. Ask forgiveness of those whom you have hurt, and forgive those who have hurt you. Hurt is way too heavy for a soul to carry around!
3. Most importantly, forgive yourself for everything you've done in the past and get on with your life! Eat chocolate and enjoy it. What the hell!
4. Find ways to help others. It will be the happiest you could ever make yourself.
5. Call or write all the people who mean something to you and tell them.
6. Plan that trip you always wanted to make and do it next year. Carpe diem!
7. Light your fireplace or some candles, play your favorite upbeat music, and dance (even if you're home alone). No one will see, and it will set you free.
8. Take a walk—on the beach or on a trail—

every chance you get. The joy will fill you up.

9. Buy a present for someone who doesn't expect anything from you.

10. Write down something you have been wanting to do, and then do it in the coming year. Thinking about it is way harder than actually doing it.

Here's an important bonus one: Be kind to one another and to ourselves this year and forever more.

Turning the Page

Why is it that the last few weeks of the year bring about a soulful mixture of blues and inspiration?

What is there to be melancholy about? Well, that's complicated. There is the fact that another year flew by. How did that happen? What I saw in the mirror was me looking another year older. However, that's really the least of my worries.

We can't help but remember past New Year's Eves and the anticipation they held. We remember what we wore and where we were. That was fun then, but now I'll be happy to be home making dinner with my husband.

At this stage of our lives, all of us are walking through minefields, so we have to be careful where we step. Some of our dear friends may not be so lucky; we don't know who or when. We didn't think like this when we were kids. But now it's a fact of life.

Just accept, adjust, and move on.

Remember, the blues ain't nuthin but a type of music!

As for the inspiration…that part is easy! Starting January 1, it's all about new beginnings: diets, exercise, to-do lists, relationships, scheduling, organization, recipes, you name it. I can't wait to see the new things and people that will inspire me. A new year always makes me feel anything is possible. I expect mostly good things (ok, maybe one or two little bad things).

A friend taught me: Write down your goals. On the left side write down the everyday things you need to do. On the right side write down your wish list. Things you dream about and long to do. This really helps you achieve them.

We need to dream it, see it, and do it. I believe we can.

Dream it, see it, do it!

The reason for the rocks and stones
Has appeared at last.
They have come to teach me.
Have patience,
Have strength they say,
Look what we have withstood.

Poem and photograph by Beverlye Hyman Fead.

About the Author

Speaker and advocate for aging and cancer Beverlye Hyman Fead writes the popular blog "Aging in High Heels." A photographer, painter, and poet in her early eighties, she is also the author of two books—*I Can Do This. Living With Cancer* and *Nana, What's Cancer?*—as well as the producer of the award-winning short documentary, *Stage IV, Living With Cancer.*

Besides writing, Beverlye enjoys seeing nature in all forms, hiking, walks on the beach, tennis, and golf. A longtime resident of Los Angeles, she now lives in Montecito, California, with her husband, Bob Fead. Between them, they have four children, five grandchildren, and a beautiful dachshund named Sophia.

CPSIA information can be obtained
at www.ICGtesting.com
Printed in the USA
FSOW01n0052120216
16822FS

9 780692 574584